Let's start!

How to use this book

Do you remember how to use this **Practice Book**?

Use the **Textbook** first to learn how to solve this type of problem.

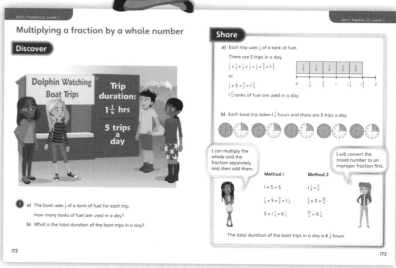

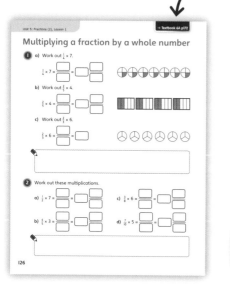

This shows you which **Textbook** page you need.

Have a go at questions by yourself using this **Practice Book**. Use what you have learnt.

Challenge questions make you think hard!

Questions with this light bulb make you think differently.

Power Maths

Year 6 Practice Book 6A

What did you like doing best in maths in Year 5?

Draw or write an example here.

This book belongs to _____ .

My class is _____ .

Pearson

Contents

I am looking forward to practising what I have learnt!

Reflect

Each lesson ends with a Reflect question so you can think about what you have learnt.

Use My Power Points at the back of this book to keep track of what you have learnt.

Reflect

Explain why $1\frac{2}{3} \times 4$ is equal to $6\frac{2}{3}$.

128

My journal

At the end of a unit your teacher will ask you to fill in My journal.

This will help you show how much you can do now that you have finished the unit.

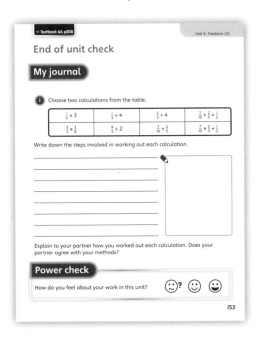

→ Textbook 6A p208

Unit 5: Fractions (2)

End of unit check

My journal

1 Choose two calculations from the table.

| $\frac{1}{5} \times 3$ | $\frac{1}{3} \div 4$ | $\frac{2}{5} \times 4$ | $\frac{7}{10} + \frac{2}{5} \times \frac{1}{2}$ |
| $\frac{2}{3} \times \frac{3}{8}$ | $\frac{4}{5} \div 2$ | $\frac{7}{10} + \frac{2}{5}$ | $\frac{7}{10} \times \frac{2}{5} + \frac{1}{2}$ |

Write down the steps involved in working out each calculation.

Explain to your partner how you worked out each calculation. Does your partner agree with your methods?

Power check

How do you feel about your work in this unit?

153

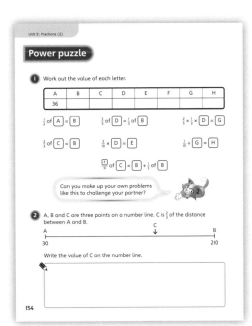

Unit 5: Fractions (2)

Power puzzle

1 Work out the value of each letter.

| A | B | C | D | E | F | G | H |
| 36 | | | | | | | |

$\frac{1}{2}$ of $\boxed{A} = \boxed{B}$

$\frac{2}{5}$ of $\boxed{D} = \frac{1}{3}$ of $\boxed{B}$

$\frac{2}{5} \times \frac{1}{3} \times \boxed{D} = \boxed{G}$

$\frac{2}{3}$ of $\boxed{C} = \boxed{B}$

$\frac{3}{10} \times \boxed{D} = \boxed{E}$

$\frac{1}{10} \div \boxed{G} = \boxed{H}$

$\frac{11}{4}$ of $\boxed{C} = \boxed{B} + \frac{1}{3}$ of $\boxed{B}$

Can you make up your own problems like this to challenge your partner?

2 A, B and C are three points on a number line. C is $\frac{2}{3}$ the distance between A and B.

A   C   B
30   ↓   210

Write the value of C on the number line.

154

→ Textbook 6A p8

Numbers to 1,000,000

1 Write the numbers that are shown on the place value grids.

a)

HTh	TTh	Th	H	T	O
●●●	●●	●●●●● ●●●●	●●●●	●	●●

b)

HTh	TTh	Th	H	T	O
	●●●●●● ●●	●●	●●●		●●●●

2 Write each of the numbers in numerals.

a) one hundred and twenty-three thousand

b) four hundred and thirty-nine thousand, two hundred and eighty-six

c) ninety-seven thousand, one hundred and three

d) three hundred and five thousand, two hundred and forty-six

6

3 What is the value of each underlined digit?

a) 731,1<u>4</u>2 _____

b) 2<u>4</u>,904 _____

c) 7,37<u>3</u> _____

d) <u>5</u>18,420 _____

e) 112,30<u>4</u> _____

f) 35,<u>1</u>82 _____

4 Using all six digit cards each time, write a number:

a) that is even

b) that is odd

c) that is a multiple of 5

d) that is greater than 500,000 but less than 700,000.

| 7 | 8 | 5 |
| 3 | 4 | 9 |

5 a) Write in the missing numbers.

330,000   370,000

300,000   400,000

b) Estimate where the number 39,411 is on the number line.

30,000   40,000

6 Write in the missing numbers. Start from the original number each time.

a)

Number	1,000 more	100 more	10 more	10 less
73,400				

b)

Number	100,000 more	10,000 more	1,000 less	1,000 more
650,167				

7 Max is thinking of a number. His number:

CHALLENGE

- is a 6-digit, odd number
- has the same number of 1,000s as 1s
- is greater than half a million
- has a digit sum of 26.

Write two numbers that could be Max's number.

[ ] and [ ]

Reflect

Write down three pieces of information about the number 172,428. Compare your information with your partner's information.

_____

_____

_____

Numbers to 10,000,000 ❶

1 How many buttons are there?

a)
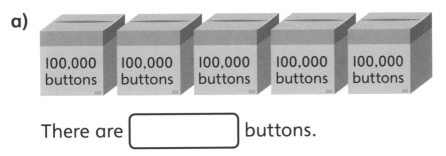

There are ⬚ buttons.

b)
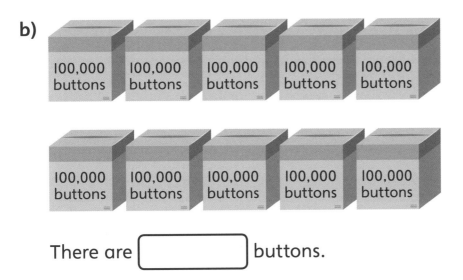

There are ⬚ buttons.

c)
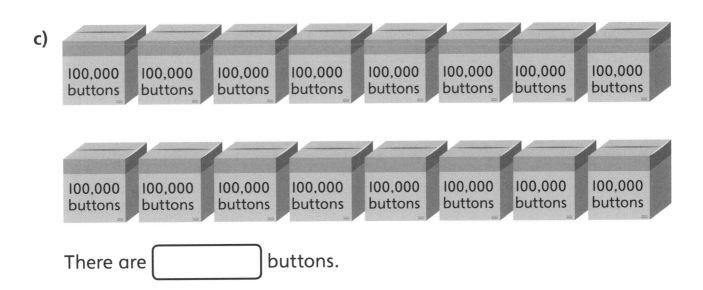

There are ⬚ buttons.

2 What numbers are shown on the place value grids?

Write each number in numerals and in words.

a)

M	HTh	TTh	Th	H	T	O
1,000,000 1,000,000	100,000 100,000 100,000 100,000 100,000 100,000 100,000 100,000 100,000		1,000 1,000 1,000	100 100 100 100	10 10 10 10 10 10 10	1

[   ] _____

_____

b)

M	HTh	TTh	Th	H	T	O
1,000,000 1,000,000 1,000,000			1,000 1,000 1,000 1,000 1,000	100 100 100 100 100 100 100	10 10 10 10 10 10	1 1 1 1 1 1

[   ] _____

_____

3 Draw counters on the place value grids to show each number.

a) 6,146,005

M	HTh	TTh	Th	H	T	O

b) five hundred and seventy thousand, two hundred and thirty

M	HTh	TTh	Th	H	T	O

4 Write each number in numerals.

a) one million, eighty-four thousand, three hundred

b) two million, two hundred and two thousand and two

c) ninety-two thousand and ninety-two

5 Write a number less than ten million that has:

- 6 as the first and last digits
- 43 thousands
- 5 hundreds
- no 10s.

6 Danny says you can tell if a number is odd or even just by knowing one of the digits. Is Danny correct? Explain your answer.

CHALLENGE

_____

_____

Reflect

Write the value of each digit in the number 8,027,361.

_____

_____

_____

→ Textbook 6A p16

Numbers to 10,000,000 ❷

1 Luis, Bella and Jamilla are playing a board game with toy money.

a) This place value grid shows Luis's money. How much does he have?

M	HTh	TTh	Th	H	T	O
£1,000,000 £1,000,000	£100,000 £100,000 £100,000	£10,000 £10,000	£1,000 £1,000 £1,000 £1,000 £1,000 £1,000	£100 £100 £100 £100	£10 £10 £10 £10 £10	£1 £1 £1 £1 £1 £1 £1
2	3	2	6	4	5	7

2,000,000 + 300,000 + 20,000 + 6,000 + ☐ + ☐ + ☐ =

☐

Luis has £☐.

b) This place value grid shows Bella's money. How much does she have?

M	HTh	TTh	Th	H	T	O
	£100,000 £100,000 £100,000	£10,000 £10,000 £10,000 £10,000 £10,000			£10 £10 £10	£1 £1 £1 £1 £1 £1 £1

☐ + ☐ + ☐ + ☐ = ☐

Bella has £☐.

c) This is Jamilla's money. How much does she have?

Jamilla has £☐.

2 Complete the part-whole models.

a)

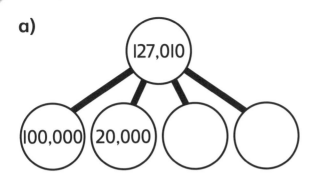

b)

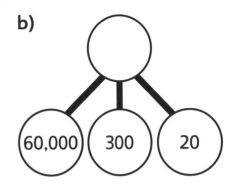

3 Complete the partitions.

a) $8,047 = 8,000 + 40 + \boxed{}$

b) $30,429 = 30,000 + \boxed{} + \boxed{} + \boxed{}$

c) $260,392 = \boxed{} + \boxed{} + \boxed{} + \boxed{} + \boxed{}$

d) $8,500 + 12 = \boxed{}$

e) $720,000 + 3,500 + 70 + 2 = \boxed{}$

f) $3,000,000 + 56,000 + 800 + 25 = \boxed{}$

g) $412 + 4,000,000 + \boxed{} = 4,412,412$

4 Complete the sentences.

a) 100 more than 3,098,728 is $\boxed{}$.

b) 1,000 more than 3,098,728 is $\boxed{}$.

c) 10,000 more than 3,098,728 is $\boxed{}$.

d) 1 million less than 3,098,728 is $\boxed{}$.

e) 100,000 less than 3,098,728 is $\boxed{}$.

5 What is the value of the underlined digit in each number?

a) 7,456,820

c) 3,307,184

_____

_____

b) 2,768,415

d) 6,000,070

_____

_____

6 What is this number? Is there more than one solution?

CHALLENGE

> The number has 7 digits.
> The ten-thousands digit is half the ones digit.
> The hundreds digit is 3 times the millions digit.
> The total of all the digits is 20.

The number is [   ].

Reflect

Write two number sentences showing how you can partition 4,508,375 in two different ways. Compare your sentences with your partner's. Discuss how they are the same or different.

_____

_____

_____

Number line to 10,000,000

1 What does each number line go up in?

a)

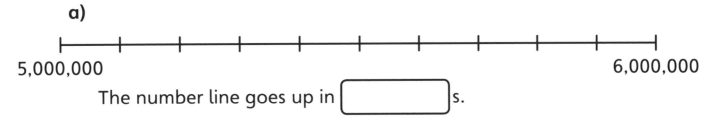

5,000,000   6,000,000

The number line goes up in [   ]s.

b)

90,000   100,000

The number line goes up in [   ]s.

2 Complete the number lines.

a)

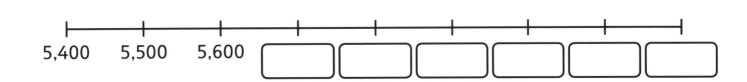

5,400   5,500   5,600   [   ] [   ] [   ] [   ] [   ] [   ]

b)

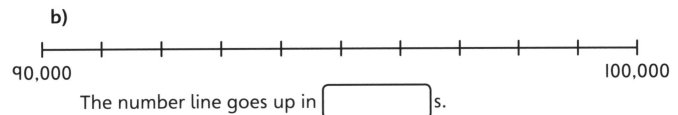

66,310   66,320   66,330   [   ] [   ] [   ]

3 Write in the missing numbers.

a) 127,520   128,520   129,520   [   ] [   ] [   ]

b) 420,700   520,700   620,700   [   ] [   ] [   ]

c) 7,400   7,300   7,200   [   ] [   ] [   ]

d) 3,200,000 3,210,000 3,220,000   [   ] [   ] [   ]

4 What numbers are the arrows pointing to?

a)

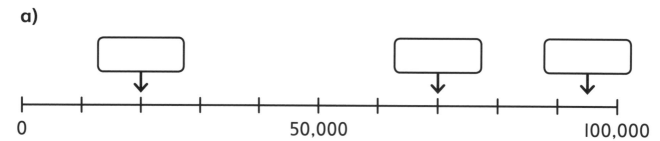

b)

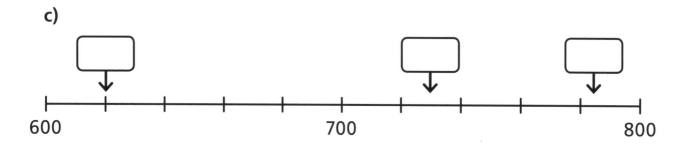

c)

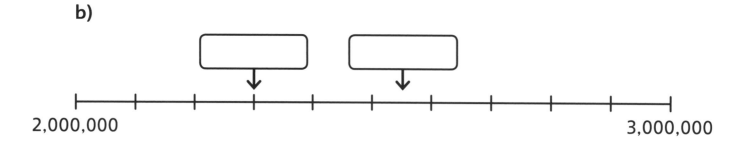

5 Draw arrows from each number to its position on the number line.

a)   815,000   870,000   851,000

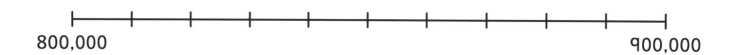

b)   9,500   9,999   8,400   8,950

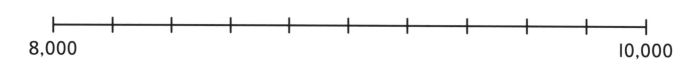

16

CHALLENGE

6 The bar chart shows the population of three countries in a particular year.

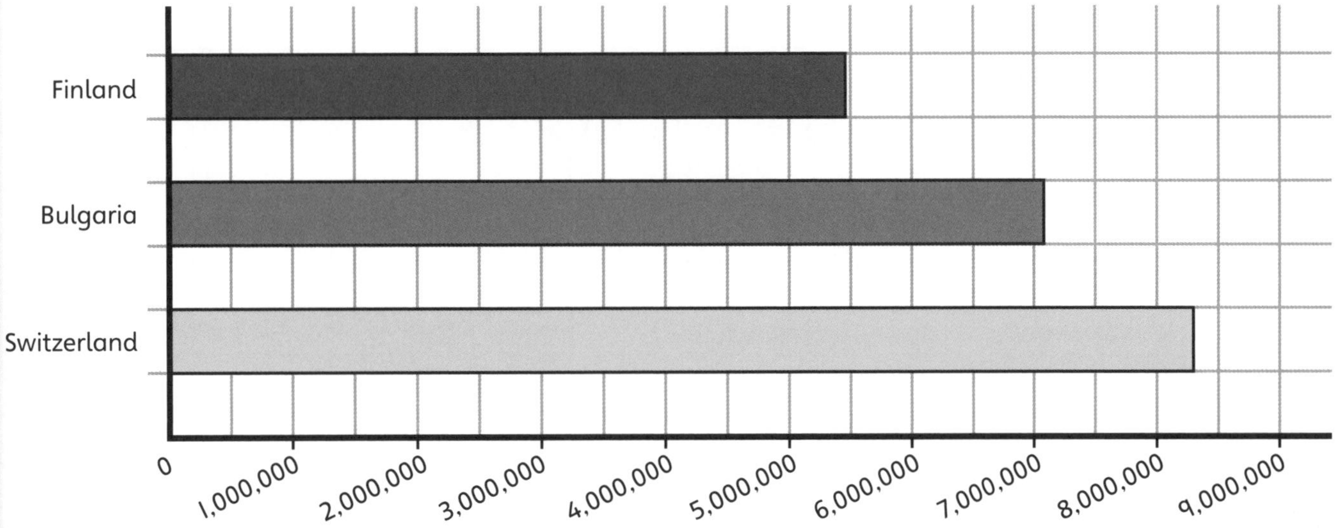

Finland
Bulgaria
Switzerland
0
1,000,000
2,000,000
3,000,000
4,000,000
5,000,000
6,000,000
7,000,000
8,000,000
9,000,000

Estimate the population of each country.

a) Finland's population is about ☐.

b) Bulgaria's population is about ☐.

c) Switzerland's population is about ☐.

Reflect

How can you estimate what number the arrow is pointing to?

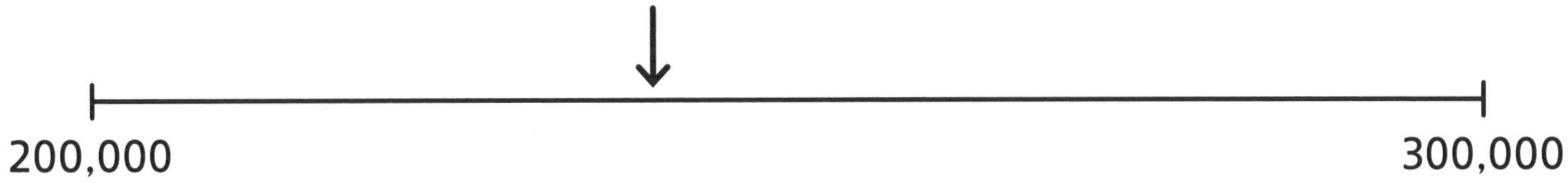

200,000
300,000

Comparing and ordering numbers to 10,000,000

1 Which number is greater, A or B? Explain your answer.

	M	HTh	TTh	Th	H	T	O
A							

	M	HTh	TTh	Th	H	T	O
B							

Number ☐ is greater, because _____

_____ .

2 Complete the number sentences using < or > .

a) 9,580 ◯ 9,570   9,580 ◯ 9,589

9,580 ◯ 9,680   9,580 ◯ 10,000

9,580 ◯ 9,681   10,000 ◯ 9,580

b) 540,000 ◯ 54,000   540,000 ◯ half a million

540,000 ◯ 450,000   540,000 ◯ 600,000

540,000 ◯ 540   540,000 ◯ 3,000,000

3 Write the letter for each house in order of price. Start with the least expensive.

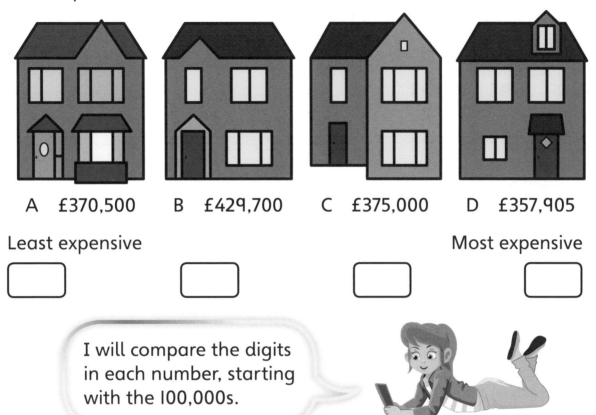

A £370,500   B £429,700   C £375,000   D £357,905

Least expensive   Most expensive

I will compare the digits in each number, starting with the 100,000s.

4 The table shows the masses of four elephants in a safari park.

The elephants are fed one at a time, in order, starting with the heaviest. Which elephant is fed third?

_____ is fed third.

Elephant	Mass
Alfie	5,600 kg
Benny	5,060 kg
Cal	6,050 kg
Dolly	5,006 kg

5 Write the following numbers in ascending order.

725,906   728,000   725,960   73,000

Smallest   Greatest

6 What could the missing digit be in each number?

Write down all the possibilities.

a) 3,☐40 < 3,270   _____

b) 2☐,390 > 25,400   _____

c) 2☐,390 > 24,380   _____

d) 8,491 > 8,4☐6   _____

e) 8,491,012 > 8,49☐,102   _____

7 Find the missing digits. Give three different answers.

CHALLENGE

246,17☐ < 24☐,1☐0 < 246,☐☐5 < 246,400

246,17☐ < 24☐,1☐0 < 246,☐☐5 < 246,400

246,17☐ < 24☐,1☐0 < 246,☐☐5 < 246,400

Reflect

These numbers are in descending order (get smaller): true or false? Explain your answer.

15,600   12,600   12,500   120,000   2,000

_____

_____

_____

Rounding numbers

1 Olivia represents the number 13,672 on a place value grid.

TTh	Th	H	T	O

a) Olivia says that to round the number to the nearest 1,000 she needs to look at the thousands column. Is Olivia correct? Explain your answer.

_____

_____

b) Complete the sentences.

13,672 rounded to the nearest 1,000 is [   ].

13,672 rounded to the nearest 100 is [   ].

2 The arrow points to a number on the number line.

Round the number to the nearest 1,000,000. Explain your answer.

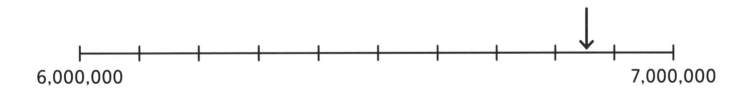

6,000,000   7,000,000

The number rounds to [   ] because _____

_____.

3 **a)** 137,987 rounded to the nearest 100,000 is [　　　].

147,987 rounded to the nearest 100,000 is [　　　].

157,987 rounded to the nearest 100,000 is [　　　].

167,987 rounded to the nearest 100,000 is [　　　].

b) 57,390 rounded to the nearest 10,000 is [　　　].

57,480 rounded to the nearest 10,000 is [　　　].

57,590 rounded to the nearest 10,000 is [　　　].

57,690 rounded to the nearest 10,000 is [　　　].

4 Complete the table.

Rounded to the nearest	128,381	1,565,900	72,308
100,000			
10,000			
1,000			
100			
10			

5 Circle the numbers that round to 17,000 to the nearest 1,000.

17,450   17,399   16,500   17,500

16,790   16,099   16,999   17,098

6

| 1 | 2 | 5 | 6 | 9 |

Use the digit cards to make a number that:

a) rounds to 15,700 to the nearest 100

b) rounds to 60,000 to the nearest 10,000

c) rounds to 60,000 to the nearest 1,000.

7 Complete the sentences.

CHALLENGE

a) 3,607 rounded to the nearest _____ is 3,610.

b) 11,53⬜ rounded to the nearest 100 is 11,500.

c) 25,497 rounded to the nearest _____ and

_____ is ⬜ .

d) 25,⬜97 rounded to the nearest 10, 100 and 1,000 is ⬜ .

Reflect

15,782 rounds to 16,000 to the nearest 1,000: true or false? Explain in two different ways how you know.

_____

_____

_____

→ Textbook 6A p32

Negative numbers

1 The table shows the temperature in three places in the UK.

Fort William	Leeds	Swansea
⁻6 °C	⁻3 °C	7 °C

a) The temperature in Fort William increases by 7 °C.

What is the new temperature?

☐ °C

b) How much colder is the temperature in Leeds than in Swansea?

☐ °C

2 Isla and Mo are playing a game. Isla is on ⁻3 and Mo is on 6.

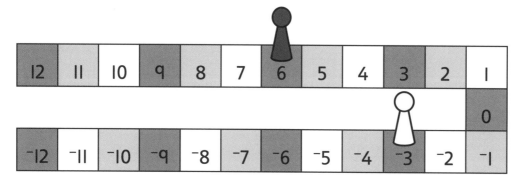

Mo moves back 7 places. Isla moves forward 10 places.

How many places ahead of Mo is Isla now?

☐ places

3 A pipe is 24 metres below ground. A crane lifts the pipe 38 metres upwards.

How many metres above the ground is the pipe now?

☐ metres

4 Complete the number lines.

a)

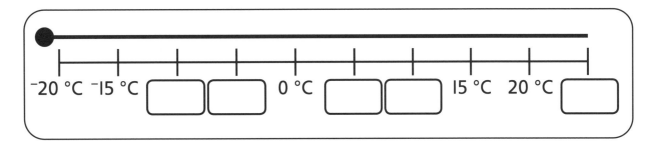

b)

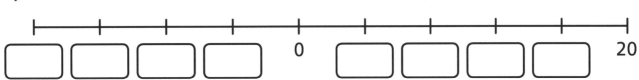

c)

5 A number line is divided into sections.

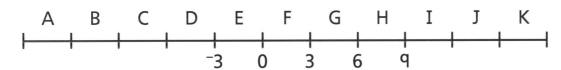

a) In which section will each of these numbers appear?

7 _____   11 _____   ⁻5 _____

17·5 _____   ⁻3½ _____   ⁻11·1 _____

b) Write down three numbers that will appear in section B.

25

6 What are the values of A and B?

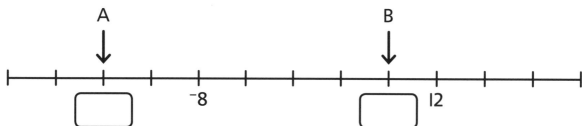

7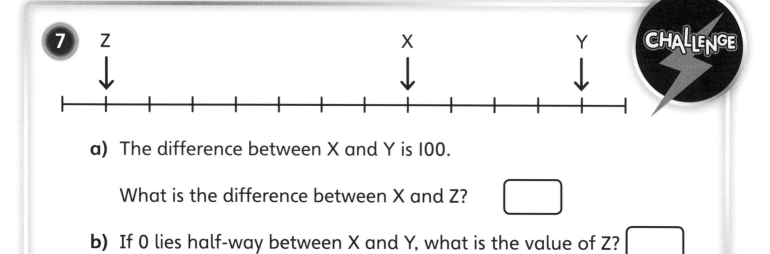

CHALLENGE

a) The difference between X and Y is 100.

What is the difference between X and Z?

b) If 0 lies half-way between X and Y, what is the value of Z?

Reflect

Explain how you can work out the values of A and B.

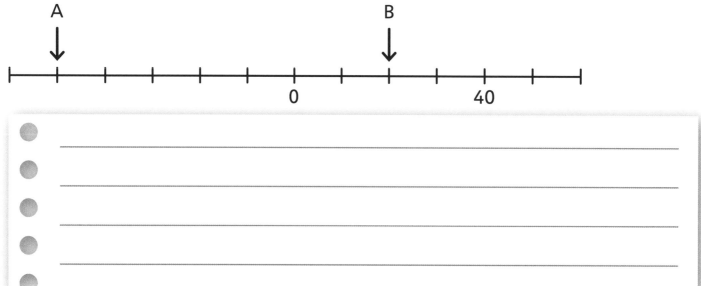

End of unit check

My journal

1. Use some or all of the digit cards to make numbers that match the statements below.

| 0 | 1 | 3 | 5 | 6 | 8 | 9 |

An even number that lies between 120,000 and 160,000.	
A number that has 3 more 100s than 10,000s.	
A number that is 10,000 more than 50,389.	
The greatest number less than seven million that you can make.	
A number that rounds to 9,000,000 to the nearest 1,000,000.	

Power check

How do you feel about your work in this unit?

Power puzzle

Use the clues below to work out what 7-digit number to write on the cards.

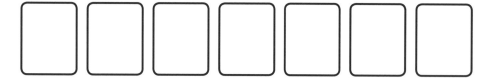

- All of the digits are different.

- The number is odd.

- The number is greater than 5 million but less than 7 million.

- The 1,000,000s digit is 4 more than the 100s digit.

- The number is not a multiple of 5.

- The sum of the first three digits is equal to the sum of the last three digits.

- The digit in the 10s column is 4 times the digit in the 100,000s column.

- The digit in the 10,000s column is 3 times the digit in the 1,000s column.

Try making up your own number puzzles like this to challenge your partner. Write clues about 4-digit, 5-digit and 6-digit numbers.

Problem solving – using written methods of addition and subtraction

1 Work out the addition.

3,214 + 564 = ⬚

Th	H	T	O
1,000 1,000 1,000	100 100	10	1 1 1 1
	100 100 100 100 100	10 10 10 10 10 10	1 1 1 1

  Th H T O
_____

+
_____

_____

2 What calculation is shown on the number line?

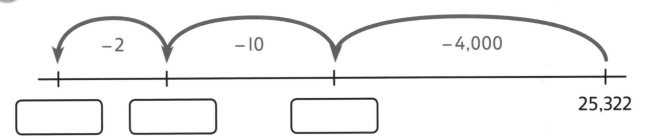

−2   −10   −4,000   25,322

⬚   ⬚   ⬚

⬚ ◯ ⬚ = ⬚

3 Solve these calculations.

a) 101,573 − 100,432 = ⬚

b) ⬚ = 234,501 + 40,078

  HTh TTh Th   H   T   O
_____

−
_____

_____

  HTh TTh Th   H   T   O
_____

+
_____

_____

4 A pilot flew 2,438 km on Monday and then 1,330 km on Tuesday.

a) How much further did she fly on Monday than on Tuesday?

b) On Wednesday, the pilot flew 227 km less than on Monday. How far did she fly on Monday, Tuesday and Wednesday in total?

5 Max is doing a column subtraction. What two mistakes has he made? What is the correct answer?

TTh	Th	H	T	O
2	5	3	9	9
–		2	3	5	1
0	3	6	4	8

6 Fill in the missing numbers.

TTh	Th	H	T	O
3	9		2	5
–		3		1
2	1	0	2	

TTh	Th	H	T	O
1		0	1	
2	4	0	1	4
+	1		2	4
9	6	0		9

7 Work out the missing numbers.

CHALLENGE

a) $9{,}999{,}999 - \boxed{} = 909{,}090$

b) $\boxed{} - 919{,}293 = 50{,}206$

Reflect

Write a story problem for the calculation $74{,}505 - \boxed{} = 21{,}200$.

→ Textbook 6A p44

Problem solving – using written methods of addition and subtraction ❷

1 Isla and Max use counters to represent different numbers.

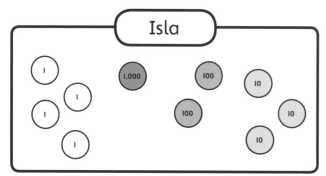

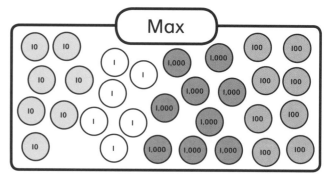

a) Reena makes the number 14,321. How much bigger is Reena's number than Isla's number?

b) How much bigger is Reena's number than Max's number and Isla's number combined?

c) Subtract 909 from each of the three numbers.

2 The Second World War ended in 1945. It started in 1939. How many years did the war last for?

Show an efficient method for working out the answer to this subtraction.

3 These numbers are on a number line. B lies half-way between A and C. What is the sum of A, B and C?

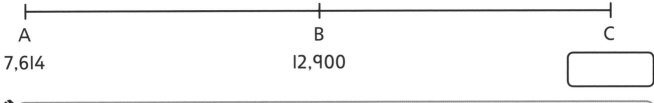

A
7,614

B
12,900

C

4 Solve these subtractions.

a) 4,321 – 1,234 =

b) 7,654,321 – 1,234,567 =

CHALLENGE

5 Amelia scored 29,750 fewer points than Bella. Bella scored 15,200 points, then 21,500 points.

How many points did they score altogether?

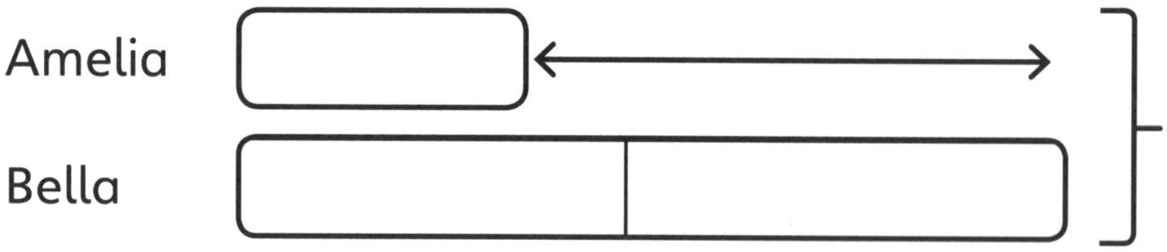

Amelia ⬚ ⟵⟶

Bella ⬚

Reflect

To work out 5,000 − 1,728, you can do 4,999 − 1,727. Explain why.

Use a similar method to work out 50,000 − 26,304.

Multiplying numbers up to 4 digits by a 1-digit number

1 Complete the multiplications. Use a different method for each one.

a) 3 × 2,324 = [ ]

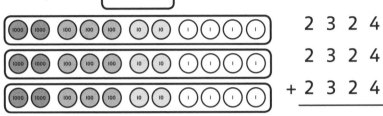

```
  2 3 2 4
  2 3 2 4
+ 2 3 2 4
_____

_____
```

b) 2,153 × 5 = [ ]

2,000	100	50	3

5

c) 5,203 × 6 = [ ]

```
  5 2 0 3
×       6
_____

_____
```

d) 7 × 1,593 = [ ]

```
×
_____

_____
```

2 Calculate the final number on the number line.

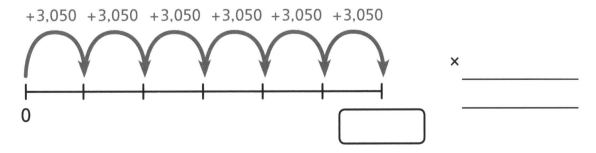

+3,050 +3,050 +3,050 +3,050 +3,050 +3,050

0

×
_____

_____

3 Complete the multiplications.

a) 251 × 7 = [ ]   **b)** 1,251 × 7 = [ ]   **c)** 1,251 × 8 = [ ]

4 Calculate the total mass of each pile of boxes.

a)

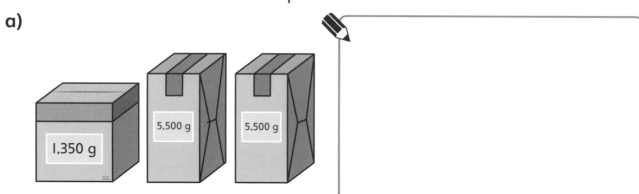

b)

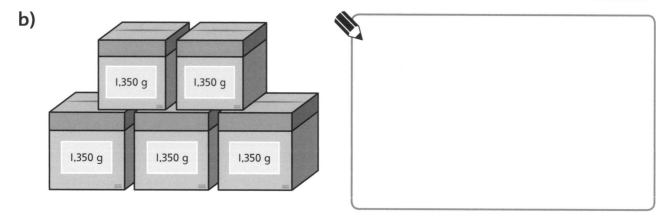

c)

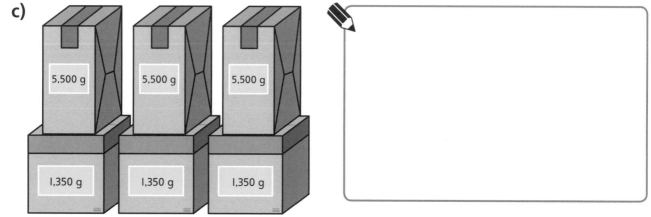

5

a) Use each digit once to complete two multiplications.

What is the difference between the two answers?

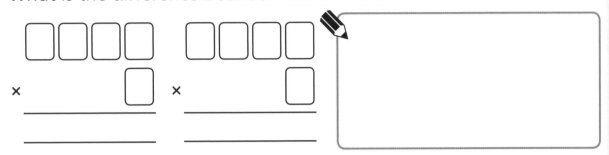

b) Max uses these cards to make a 4-digit number and a 1-digit number. He multiplies them together. What is the biggest number he can make? What is the smallest number he can make?

| 5 | 6 | 7 | 8 | 9 |

Reflect

Explain how these two multiplication methods are related.

→ Textbook 6A p52

Multiplying numbers up to 4 digits by a 2-digit number

 Complete the multiplications.

a) 3,125 × 15 = ☐

```
    3  1  2  5
×         1  5
─────────────────
       2  5       5 × 5
    1  0  0       5 × 20
    5  0  0       5 × 100
 1  5  0  0  0    5 × 3,000
                  10 × 5
                  10 × 20
                  10 × 100
                  10 × 3,000
─────────────────
─────────────────
```

	3,000	100	20	5
10				
5	15,000	500	100	25

b) 5,123 × 13 = ☐

	5,000	100	20	3
10				
3				

```
    5  1  2  3
×         1  3
─────────────────
                  3 × 5,123
                  10 × 5,123
─────────────────
```

c) 1,972 × 24 = ☐

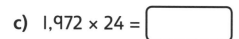

2 **a)** In 2021, there will be 365 days in the year. How many hours will there be?

b) There are 3,600 seconds in an hour. How many seconds are there in a day?

3 Richard is working out 5,056 × 14. He says he will work out 5,056 × 7, and then double the result.

Check if his method works then explain what you find.

```
    5 0 5 6              5 0 5 6              5 0 5 6
  ×         7          ×         2          ×       1 4
  _____          _____          _____

  _____          _____
                                            _____
```

_____

_____

4 A pool holds 8,400 litres of water. A builder fills up the pool with a 17 litre container. He pours in 379 containers of water. Is this enough to fill the pool?

5 Work out the missing digits in 3,62☐ × ☐5 = 199,595.

CHALLENGE

Reflect

Which is larger: 1,254 × 21 or 2,508 × 11? Show how you worked this out.

Dividing numbers up to 4 digits by a 2-digit number

1 Match each division to a model, and then complete the models and the divisions.

$$6 \,\overline{|\ 1\ \ 5\ \ 3\ \ 6}$$

$$1{,}536 \div 6 = \boxed{}$$

10	5	1
160	80	16

$$16 \,\overline{|\ 2\ \ 5\ \ 6}$$

$$256 \div 16 = \boxed{}$$

100	20
6,000	1,200

$$16 \,\overline{|\ 3\ \ 6\ \ 0\ \ 0}$$

$$3{,}600 \div 16 = \boxed{}$$

6

200	50	6
1,200	300	36

$$60 \,\overline{|\ 7\ \ 2\ \ 0\ \ 0}$$

$$\boxed{} = 7{,}200 \div 60$$

200	20	5
3,200	320	

2 Complete these divisions.

a)

$$33 \overline{)\ 7\ \ 5\ \ 9\ }$$

$759 \div 33 = \boxed{}$

b)

$$14 \overline{)\ 2\ \ 9\ \ 5\ \ 4\ }$$

$2{,}954 \div 14 = \boxed{}$

3 Max has 3,500 g of guinea pig food to last for 25 days. How much food can he use per day?

4 Solve these divisions.

a) $468 \div 9 = \boxed{}$

b) $4{,}689 \div 9 = \boxed{}$

c) $378 \div 18 = \boxed{}$

d) $3{,}798 \div 18 = \boxed{}$

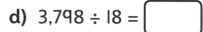

5 Fill in the missing digits.

CHALLENGE

```
      3    3
22 | 8  8
```

[ ] ÷ 22 = [ ]

```
      1    4
21 | 6    9  4
```

[ ] ÷ 21 = [ ]

Reflect

Show two methods you can use to solve 1,887 ÷ 17 = [ ].

→ Textbook 6A p60

Dividing numbers up to 4 digits by a 2-digit number ❷

1 **a)** Reena has shared 3,500 ml of juice equally between 14 glasses.
How much juice is in each glass?

| 3,500 |

$3,500 \div 7 = \boxed{}$

$\boxed{} \div 2 = \boxed{}$

$$7 \overline{\smash{)}3\ 5\ 0\ 0}$$

$$2 \overline{\smash{)}}$$

$3,500 \div 14 = \boxed{}$

b) Aki has 360 g of clay. He makes small clay shells.
Each shell weighs 24 g. How many shells can he make?

| 360 |

$360 \div 6 = \boxed{}$

$\boxed{} \div 4 = \boxed{}$

2 Complete the divisions.

1,260 ⟶ ⸳÷ 10⸳ ⟶ ⸳÷ 2⸳ ⟶   1,260 ÷ 20 = ▢

180 ⟶ ⸳÷ 3⸳ ⟶ ⸳÷ 5⸳ ⟶   180 ÷ 15 = ▢

960 ⟶ ⸳÷ 2⸳ ⟶ ⸳÷⸳ ⟶   960 ÷ 16 = ▢

1,100 ⟶ ⸳÷⸳ ⟶ ⸳÷⸳ ⟶   1,100 ÷ 22 = ▢

3 Complete the divisions by choosing factors.

a) 2,700 ÷ 18 = ▢

c) 5,400 ÷ 36 = ▢

b) 7,200 ÷ 12 = ▢

d) 5,600 ÷ 14 = ▢

4 **a)** 480 ÷ 8 = 60

Use division by factors to show how you can use this calculation to work out:

i) 480 ÷ 16 = ☐

ii) 960 ÷ 32 = ☐

b) Ambika says 'If I double the number that I am dividing by, the answer to the division will be halved.'

Bella says 'I think that means that if I double both numbers in a division, the answer will be halved and then halved again.'

Do you agree with both Ambika and Bella? Show how you know.

Reflect

Show two ways to work out 6,440 ÷ 20 using division by factors.

Dividing numbers up to 4 digits by a 2-digit number ❸

1 Solve these divisions.

a) $399 \div 19 = \boxed{}$

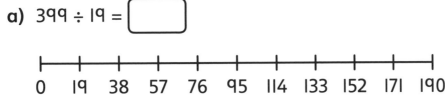

0   19   38   57   76   95   114   133   152   171   190

```
19 | 3  9  9
      1  9  0   10
     ─────────
      2  0  9
      1  9  0   10
     ─────────
```

	10	10	
19	190	190	

b) $385 \div 11 = \boxed{}$

11		

c) $888 \div 37 = \boxed{}$

37	

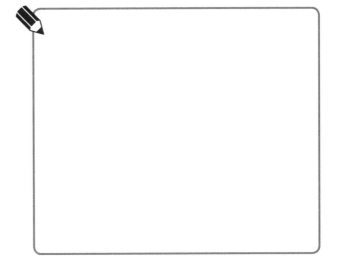

2 There are 992 pupils in a school. They are organised into classes with 31 pupils in each class. How many classes are there?

3 Complete these divisions.

a) $182 \div 13 =$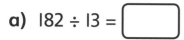

c) $528 \div 11 =$

b) $364 \div 13 =$

d) $528 \div 22 =$

4　Mo and Olivia are dividing 1,221 by 37. Mo uses three subtractions and Olivia uses five subtractions. Show their possible calculations.

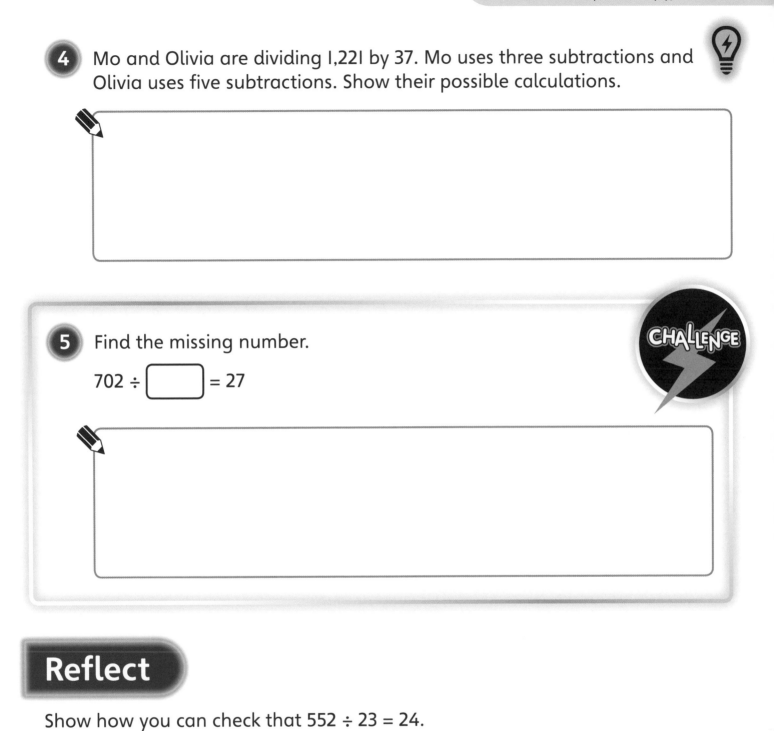

5　Find the missing number.

702 ÷ ☐ = 27

CHALLENGE

Reflect

Show how you can check that 552 ÷ 23 = 24.

→ Textbook 6A p68

Dividing numbers up to 4 digits by a 2-digit number ④

1 Work out these divisions. Use the number line to help you.

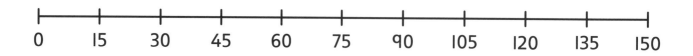

0   15   30   45   60   75   90   105   120   135   150

a)   15) 7 3 5

b)   15) 1 8 9 0

c)   15) 5 6 1 0

2 There are 1,331 footballers at a football tournament. There are 11 players in each team. How many teams will there be?

1,331 ÷ 11 = ☐

3 Jen cycles 2,444 kilometres in 26 days. Toshi cycles 2,325 kilometres in 25 days. Who cycles more kilometres per day?

4 Ebo is working out $8,845 \div 61$. He lists his multiples.

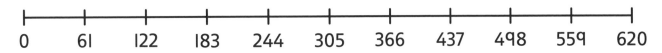

| 0 | 61 | 122 | 183 | 244 | 305 | 366 | 437 | 498 | 559 | 620 |

a) How do you know Ebo has made a mistake? Find his first mistake and correct it.

_____

_____

b) Work out the answer to the division.

5 Reena thinks she can use 2,790 ÷ 31 to work out some other related divisions. Solve 2,790 ÷ 31 and use it to complete Reena's mind map.

CHALLENGE

5,580 ÷ 31 = ☐

2,790 ÷ 62 = ☐

☐ ÷ 31 = 30

2,790 ÷ 31 = ☐

279 ÷ ☐ = 9

558 ÷ 31 = ☐

☐ ÷ 31 = 27

Reflect

Circle the division that you would not solve using division by factors. Explain why. Solve each division.

1,440 ÷ 30   2,553 ÷ 23

Dividing numbers up to 4 digits by a 2-digit number ⑤

1 Emma and Aki are discussing divisions. Show who is correct.

Emma

 Aki

When I divide 100 by 13 I get a remainder of 9, so when I divide 100 by 14, the remainder will be 10.

When I divide 100 by 13 I get a remainder of 9, so when I divide 101 by 13 I will get a remainder of 10.

2 Andy has 200 football stickers for his album. It takes 15 stickers to fill one page. How many pages can he fill? How many stickers will be left over?

3 Draw lines to match each division to a remainder. Some remainders belong to more than one division.

$450 \div 20$

$301 \div 10$

$955 \div 50$

$685 \div 25$

$335 \div 33$

1

5

10

4 Complete these divisions, including any remainders.

a) $300 \div 11 = \boxed{}$

b) $300 \div 31 = \boxed{}$

c) $750 \div 17 = \boxed{}$

d) $850 \div 17 = \boxed{}$

5 A ranger at a wildlife reserve needs 475 kg of bird seed to make feeders. The seed comes in bags of 35 kg. How many bags will the ranger need to buy?

6 Complete this division so that it has a remainder of 40. Explain your thinking.

CHALLENGE

$\boxed{} \div 41$

_____

_____

_____

Reflect

Reena works out $300 \div 21$ by dividing by 3 and then dividing by 7. She says the remainder is 2, because $100 \div 7$ has a remainder of 2.

Is Reena correct? Explore her method and explain what you find.

_____

_____

_____

→ Textbook 6A p76

Dividing numbers up to 4 digits by a 2-digit number ⑥

1 **a)** Amelia has 2,000 ml of juice. She fills each ice-lolly mould with 75 ml of juice. How many ice lollies can she make, and how much juice will be left?

b) Bella has 2,500 ml of juice and she uses 95 ml of juice for each ice lolly. Will she have more or less juice left than Amelia?

c) What fraction of an ice lolly can Amelia and Bella each make with their remaining juice?

2 Complete these divisions.

a) $1,000 \div 11 = \boxed{}$

c) $4,000 \div 22 = \boxed{}$

b) $2,000 \div 11 = \boxed{}$

d) $8,000 \div 22 = \boxed{}$

Explain how the divisions are related and explore the pattern in the answers and the remainders.

_____

_____

3 A school receives £2,515 for new computer equipment. The money is shared equally between 20 classes in the school. How much money does each class get in pounds and pence?

4 Use each digit card once to make a division. Find the division that will give you the biggest remainder.

CHALLENGE

| 1 | 1 | 3 | 5 | 7 | 9 | ⬚ ⬚ ⬚ ⬚ ÷ ⬚ ⬚

Reflect

Write a story problem that requires a division and leaves a remainder of 10.

_____

_____

_____

End of unit check

My journal

1

Use the digit cards to create one of these multiplications.

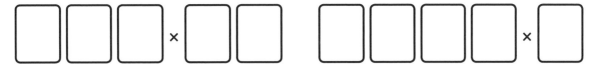

Divide the answer to your multiplication by 25.

Now, try to make a multiplication with an answer that leaves a remainder of 10 when you divide it by 25.

Power check

How do you feel about your work in this unit?

Power puzzle

Subtraction trap!

Choose any four digits.

I choose 2, 1, 8 and 4.

↓

Make the largest possible number. Make the smallest possible number.

The largest number is 8,421. The smallest number is 1,248.

↓

Find the difference between your two numbers.

Th	H	T	O
8	³4	¹¹2̶	¹1
− 1	2	4	8
7	1	7	3

↓

The answer gives you four new digits.

↓

Start again with these four digits.

Now I start again with the digits 7, 1, 7 and 3.

Keep going. Did you end up repeating yourself? How long did your chain last?

Try different starting numbers. Compare your results with everyone in your class.

Common factors

1 **a)** Use these arrays to find all the factors of 14 and 18.

○○○○○○○○○○○○○○ $\boxed{} \times \boxed{} = 14$

○○○○○○○
○○○○○○○ $\boxed{} \times \boxed{} = 14$

○○○○○○○○○○○○○○○○○○ $\boxed{} \times \boxed{} = 18$

○○○○○○○○○
○○○○○○○○○ $\boxed{} \times \boxed{} = 18$

○○○○○○
○○○○○○
○○○○○○ $\boxed{} \times \boxed{} = 18$

The factors of 14 are $\boxed{}$, $\boxed{}$, $\boxed{}$ and $\boxed{}$.

The factors of 18 are $\boxed{}$, $\boxed{}$, $\boxed{}$, $\boxed{}$, $\boxed{}$

and $\boxed{}$.

b) List the common factors of 14 and 18.

The common factors of 14 and 18 are $\boxed{}$ and $\boxed{}$.

c) Draw a diagram to show why 6 is **not** a common factor of 14 and 18.

I will try to draw an array like those in part a).

2 Complete these lists, then find the common factors of 40 and 100.

$1 \times \boxed{} = 40$ $\qquad\qquad$ $1 \times \boxed{} = 100$

$\boxed{} \times \boxed{} = 40$ _____

$\boxed{} \times \boxed{} = 40$ _____

$\boxed{} \times \boxed{} = 40$ _____

_____

The common factors of 40 and 100 are _____ .

3 Max has made **two** mistakes. Find them and prove they are mistakes.

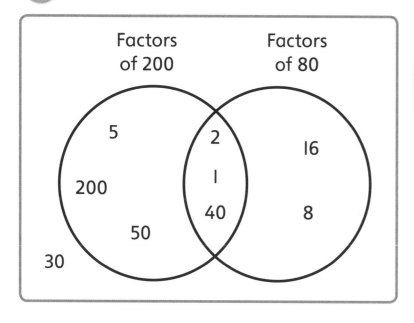

I wonder if all the factors of 80 and 200 are here? I could add some more.

$\boxed{}$ is in the wrong place because _____

_____ .

$\boxed{}$ is in the wrong place because _____

_____ .

4 **a)** Complete the table to show all the factors of 35, 50 and 70.

Factors of 35	Factors of 50	Factors of 70

Circle the common factors of all three numbers.

b) Lexi thinks of three numbers that have the common factors 1, 2, 3, 4 and 5. What could Lexi's numbers be?

_____

Reflect

Find all the common factors of 15 and 60.

Do you need to check all the numbers up to 60?

_____
_____
_____

→ Textbook 6A p88

Common multiples

1 On the 100 square, multiples of 8 have been circled.

Shade all the multiples of 6.

Then list the common multiples of 6 and 8.

The common multiples of 6 and 8 up to 100 are ☐, ☐, ☐ and ☐.

1	2	3	4	5	6	7	⑧	9	10
11	12	13	14	15	⑯	17	18	19	20
21	22	23	㉔	25	26	27	28	29	30
31	㉜	33	34	35	36	37	38	39	㊵
41	42	43	44	45	46	47	㊽	49	50
51	52	53	54	55	㊽	57	58	59	60
61	62	63	㊽	65	66	67	68	69	70
71	㊁	73	74	75	76	77	78	79	㊽
81	82	83	84	85	86	87	㊶	89	90
91	92	93	94	95	㊽	97	98	99	100

2 **a)** Circle the common multiples of 3 and 7 on the 100 square.

1	2	3	4	5	6	7	8	9	10
11	12	13	14	15	16	17	18	19	20
21	22	23	24	25	26	27	28	29	30
31	32	33	34	35	36	37	38	39	40
41	42	43	44	45	46	47	48	49	50
51	52	53	54	55	56	57	58	59	60
61	62	63	64	65	66	67	68	69	70
71	72	73	74	75	76	77	78	79	80
81	82	83	84	85	86	87	88	89	90
91	92	93	94	95	96	97	98	99	100

b) Circle the common multiples of 5 and 15 on the 100 square.

1	2	3	4	5	6	7	8	9	10
11	12	13	14	15	16	17	18	19	20
21	22	23	24	25	26	27	28	29	30
31	32	33	34	35	36	37	38	39	40
41	42	43	44	45	46	47	48	49	50
51	52	53	54	55	56	57	58	59	60
61	62	63	64	65	66	67	68	69	70
71	72	73	74	75	76	77	78	79	80
81	82	83	84	85	86	87	88	89	90
91	92	93	94	95	96	97	98	99	100

3 Write these numbers on the sorting diagram.

40, 15, 16, 60, 6, 20, 30, 45, 100

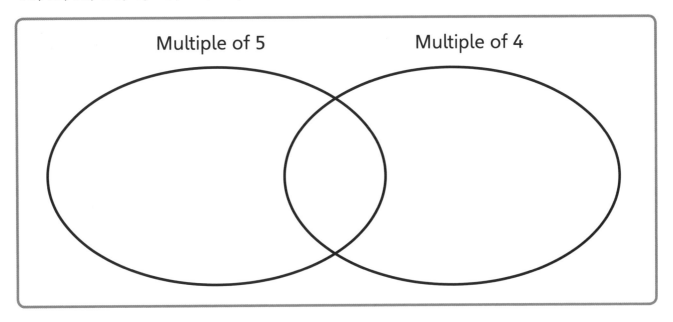

Describe what you notice about all the numbers that are common multiples of 4 and 5.

I notice that all the common multiples of 4 and 5 _____

_____

_____ .

4 List all the common multiples of 20 and 30 between 200 and 400.

5 Andy says: 'My bar model shows that 48 is a common multiple of 4 and 12. I worked out that 48 and 96 are the only common multiples of 4 and 12 up to 100.'

CHALLENGE

48

12	12	12	12

48

4	4	4	4	4	4	4	4	4	4	4	4

a) Explain how Andy's bar model shows that 48 is a common multiple of 4 and 12.

_____

_____

b) Has Andy found all the common multiples of 4 and 12 up to 100? Explain.

_____

_____

Reflect

Find three different common multiples of 20 and 25.

Explain how you found them.

_____

_____

_____

Recognising prime numbers up to 100

1 Draw an array to prove that 49 is not a prime number.

This proves that 49 is not prime because it shows that

$49 ÷ \boxed{} = \boxed{}$.

So, factors of 49 are $\boxed{}$, $\boxed{}$ and $\boxed{}$.

2 Check whether 51, 53 and 55 are prime numbers.

I know $\boxed{}$ is not a prime number because _____

_____ .

I know $\boxed{}$ is not a prime number because _____

_____ .

$\boxed{}$ is a prime number because _____

_____ .

3 Complete this 100 square by circling all the prime numbers from 20 to 100.

1	②	③	4	⑤	6	⑦	8	9	10
⑪	12	⑬	14	15	16	⑰	18	⑲	20
21	22	23	24	25	26	27	28	29	30
31	32	33	34	35	36	37	38	39	40
41	42	43	44	45	46	47	48	49	50
51	52	53	54	55	56	57	58	59	60
61	62	63	64	65	66	67	68	69	70
71	72	73	74	75	76	77	78	79	80
81	82	83	84	85	86	87	88	89	90
91	92	93	94	95	96	97	98	99	100

4 Write two numbers in each section of the table.

	Factor of 100	Not a factor of 100
Prime number		
Not a prime number		

Which section can have no more numbers in it?

_____

5 '23 is a prime number, so 123 and 223 must be prime numbers too.'

Do you agree?

Explain or show your reasoning.

CHALLENGE

Reflect

Explain how to show whether 85 and 89 are prime numbers.

→ **Textbook 6A p96**

Squares and cubes

1 Circle the correct answer for each question.

a) 7^2 is equal to:

72   14   49   9

$7 \times 7 = \boxed{}$

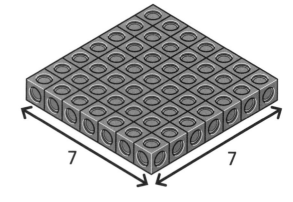

b) 5^3 is equal to:

53   125   15   25

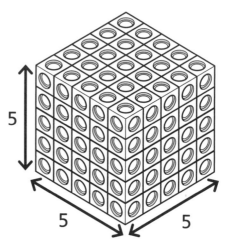

2 Add to these arrays so that they represent the written numbers.

a) 6^2

b) 10^2

3 Write in the missing numbers.

a) $9^2 = \boxed{}$

b) $10^2 = \boxed{}$

c) $11^2 = \boxed{}$

d) $\boxed{}^2 = 64$

e) $16 = \boxed{}^2$

f) $64 = \boxed{}^3$

g) $\boxed{}^2 = 1$

h) $\boxed{} = 1^3$

i) $100 = 10^{\boxed{}}$

4 How many more cubes need to be added so that this represents $6 \times 6 \times 6$?

Explain your answer.

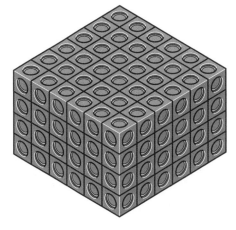

$\boxed{}$ more cubes need to be added, because _____

_____

_____ .

5 Is Bella correct? Explain.

_____

_____

_____

_____

I know $3^2 = 9$, so I think that $30^2 = 90$.

6 Write these numbers in the correct places on the sorting diagram.

4, 13, 2, 14, 64, 81, 100, 9, 91, 16

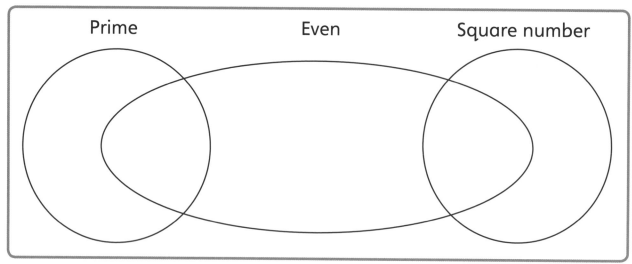

Explain why the 'prime' and 'square number' circles do not need to overlap.

_____

_____

Reflect

Find and correct the errors in Danny's work.

$1^2 = 2$ $3 = 9^2$ $5^3 = 15$

Write a comment to help him understand the mistakes he has made.

_____

_____

_____

Order of operations

1 Draw lines to match each calculation to the equipment that represents it correctly.

$$3 \times 2 + 6 \qquad 3 + 2 \times 6 \qquad 3 \times 6 + 2$$

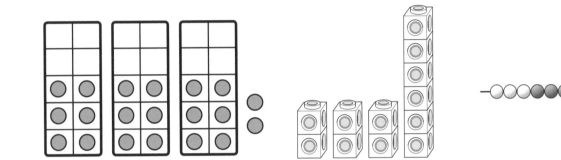

2 Draw counters that represent the correct way to solve these calculations.

a) $5 + 1 \times 5$

b) $5 \times 2 - 5$

3 Find the solution to these calculations. The first one has been started for you.

a) $\boxed{3 \times 12} - 3$

$\downarrow \qquad \downarrow$

$\boxed{} - 3 = \boxed{}$

b) $20 + 20 \times 7$

c) $10 - 2 \times 4$

d) $100 \times 8 - 8$

e) $5 \times 10 - 5$

f) $64 - 7 \times 8$

4 Find the solution to these pairs of calculations.

a) $30 + 30 \div 5 = \boxed{}$ $\qquad$ $30 \times 30 \div 5 = \boxed{}$

b) $40 + 40 \div 5 = \boxed{}$ $\qquad$ $40 \times 40 \div 5 = \boxed{}$

c) $50 + 50 \div 5 = \boxed{}$ $\qquad$ $50 \div 50 \times 5 = \boxed{}$

d) $100 + 100 \div 5 = \boxed{}$ $\qquad$ $100 \div 100 \times 5 = \boxed{}$

5 **a)** Write in the missing numbers.

$$\boxed{} + 10 \times 5 = 100$$

$$100 = 10 + \boxed{} \times 5$$

$$100 - \boxed{} \div 5 = 0$$

b) Write four different solutions to this calculation.

$$100 - \boxed{} \div \boxed{} + 100 = 199$$

$$100 - \boxed{} \div \boxed{} + 100 = 199$$

$$100 - \boxed{} \div \boxed{} + 100 = 199$$

$$100 - \boxed{} \div \boxed{} + 100 = 199$$

Explain what you notice about the pairs of missing numbers.

_____

_____

_____

CHALLENGE

Reflect

Write your own calculation that could have one wrong answer and one correct answer. Then show the order needed to complete it correctly.

_____

_____

_____

→ **Textbook 6A p104**

Brackets

1 Match each calculation to the correct representation.

10 + (2 × 3)

(10 + 2) × 3

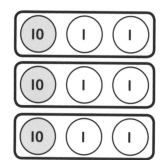

3 + (2 × 10)

?

10	3	3

2 Complete each calculation.

a) (14 + 11) × 4 = ☐

☐ ◯ ☐ = ☐

c) 3 × (50 − 25) = ☐

b) (100 − 1) ÷ 11 = ☐

d) 100 = (☐ + 17) × 5

3 A4 paper costs £3 per pack. A3 paper costs £5 per pack.

a) Mr Lopez needs to buy 12 packs of A4 paper and 12 packs of A3 paper.

Circle the calculation that finds the total cost.

$12 \times (5 \times 3)$ $(12 \times 5) + (3 \times 5)$ $5 + (3 \times 12)$ $12 \times (3 + 5)$

b) Toshi needs 15 packs of each size of paper.

Add brackets so that this calculation finds the correct cost.

$3 + 5 \times 15 = $ ⬚

c) Miss Hall buys 5 packs of A4 and 3 packs of A3.

Write a number sentence for the cost of what she bought.

_____

4 Write the correct sign >, < or = in each of the following calculations.

a) $(11 + 6) - 9$ ◯ $(11 + 6) - 5$

b) $5 \times (12 + 5)$ ◯ $(5 \times 12) + 5$

c) $(14 \times 4) \div 2$ ◯ $14 \times (4 \div 2)$

5 Add brackets and operations to make these calculations correct.

a) 2 ◯ 2 ◯ 2 ◯ $2 = 12$

b) $10 = 3$ ◯ 3 ◯ 3 ◯ 3

a) What different results can you make by inserting operations and brackets into this table? Create three different calculations for each column.

 CHALLENGE

Greater than 100	Between 0 and 1, including 0 and 1	Less than 0
10 ◯ 10 ◯ 10 ◯ 10 = [　　　]	10 ◯ 10 ◯ 10 ◯ 10 = [　　　]	10 ◯ 10 ◯ 10 ◯ 10 = [　　　]
10 ◯ 10 ◯ 10 ◯ 10 = [　　　]	10 ◯ 10 ◯ 10 ◯ 10 = [　　　]	10 ◯ 10 ◯ 10 ◯ 10 = [　　　]
10 ◯ 10 ◯ 10 ◯ 10 = [　　　]	10 ◯ 10 ◯ 10 ◯ 10 = [　　　]	10 ◯ 10 ◯ 10 ◯ 10 = [　　　]

b) What are the largest and the smallest results you can find?

Largest [　　　]   Smallest [　　　]

Reflect

Add brackets to make this calculation correct.

$10 \times 3 + 4 > 10 \times 4 + 3$

Explain how you know you have correctly placed the brackets.

_____

_____

_____

Mental calculations

1 Solve these calculations using mental methods.

a) $9 + 19 + 29 =$ ☐

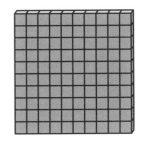

b) $4 \times 99 =$ ☐

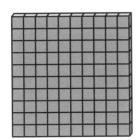 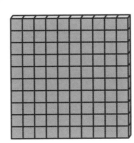 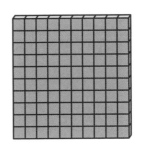

c) $35 \times 9 =$ ☐

$10 \times 35 =$ ☐

| 35 | 35 | 35 | 35 | 35 | 35 | 35 | 35 | 35 | 35 |

?

2 a) Kate spends £4·99 + £2·99 + £1·99.

How much change does she receive from a £10 note?

Kate receives ☐ change.

b) Ebo buys 5 bottles of water for 95p each. He pays with a £20 note.

What is the total cost? How much change does he receive?

Ebo spends ☐ in total. He receives ☐ change.

3 Solve these calculations. Use mental methods and jottings to support your thinking.

a) $\boxed{} = 50 \times 7 - 150$

b) $50 + 8 \times 25 = \boxed{}$

c) $(75 \times 3) + (25 \times 3) = \boxed{}$

d) $(75 \div 3) \times 9 = \boxed{}$

4 Sofia has 6 lengths of wood that are each 98 cm long. She has mentally calculated that she has 5 m and 94 cm of wood in total.

Explain why Sofia is incorrect and the mistake she has made.

_____

_____

I think she first worked out 6 × 100.

5 Draw diagrams explaining different mental methods for working out the two missing numbers.

CHALLENGE

| 49 | 49 | 49 | 49 | 49 | 49 | 49 | 49 | 49 |

| 25 | 25 | 25 | 25 | 25 | 25 | 25 | 25 | 25 |

?

?

Reflect

Suggest three things to look out for when deciding whether to calculate mentally.

→ **Textbook 6A p112**

Mental calculations ❷

 a) Max has 250 'one thousand' place value counters. He drops 20 of them. What number do the remaining counters represent?

250 – 20 = ▢

1,000

250,000 – 20,000 = ▢

The remaining counters represent two hundred and

_____ .

b) Ambika has 115 'one thousand' place value counters. She finds 5 more. What number can she represent now?

115 ◯ 5 = ▢

115,000 ◯ ▢ = ▢

Now Ambika can represent _____ .

2 Complete these calculations mentally.

a) 254,000 + 100,000 = ▢

b) Two thousand less than ninety-five thousand

is _____ .

c) The difference between two hundred thousand and half a million

is _____ .

d) 5,205,500 – 2,000,000 = ▢

3 Write the missing numbers.

a)

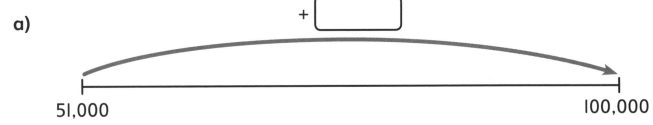

b)

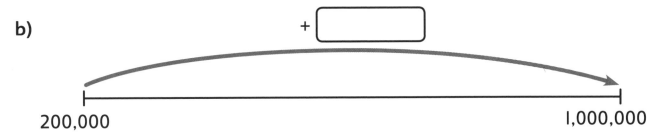

c)

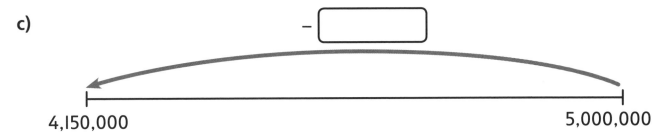

4 Solve these calculations.

a) $1{,}000 - 100 =$ ⬚

c) $1{,}000 -$ ⬚ $= 995$

b) $10{,}000 - 1{,}000 =$ ⬚

d) $20{,}000 - 1{,}000 =$ ⬚

5 Complete the table. Start with the same number each time.

1,000 less	100 less	Number	100 more	1,000 more
		100,001		
		1,000,001		
899,500				
				10,101

6 **a)** What is Mrs Dean's starting number?

CHALLENGE

> I am thinking of a number. I add 100 and then double the result. After that, I subtract a quarter of a million. My final number is one more than 599,999.

b) What could Mr Jones's starting number be?

> I am thinking of a number. I subtract 10, halve the result and then take away half a million. My final number is greater than four hundred thousand, but less than half a million.

Reflect

Write two calculations using large numbers that can be solved mentally.

Write one calculation that is difficult to solve mentally. Explain why this one is difficult to solve mentally.

Reasoning from known facts

1 Use 1-digit numbers to complete each calculation.

a) $\boxed{} \times \boxed{} \times 7 = 210$

$\downarrow$

30 $\times 7 = 210$

c) $\boxed{} \times \boxed{} \times \boxed{} = 189$

21 $\times$ 9 $= 189$

b) $\boxed{} \times \boxed{} \times \boxed{} = 150$

$\downarrow$

6 $\times$ 25 $= 150$

d) $\boxed{} \times \boxed{} \times \boxed{} = 280$

2 Use the known facts to complete the related calculations.

a)

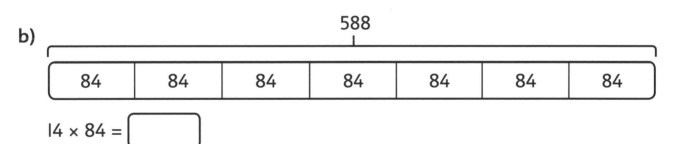

425

| 85 | 85 | 85 | 85 | 85 |

$5 \times 85 = 425$, so $6 \times 85 = \boxed{} + \boxed{} = \boxed{}$

b)

588

| 84 | 84 | 84 | 84 | 84 | 84 | 84 |

$14 \times 84 = \boxed{}$

c)

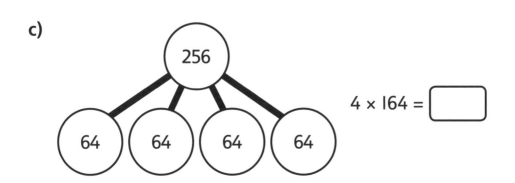

$4 \times 164 = \boxed{}$

3 Jamilla knows that 48 × 6 = 288.

She says: 'So I know 148 × 6 is 28,800 because I multiplied by 100.'

Explain Jamilla's mistake and how she can use the known fact to work out the answer correctly.

_____

_____

_____

4 **a)** Complete the related facts mind map.

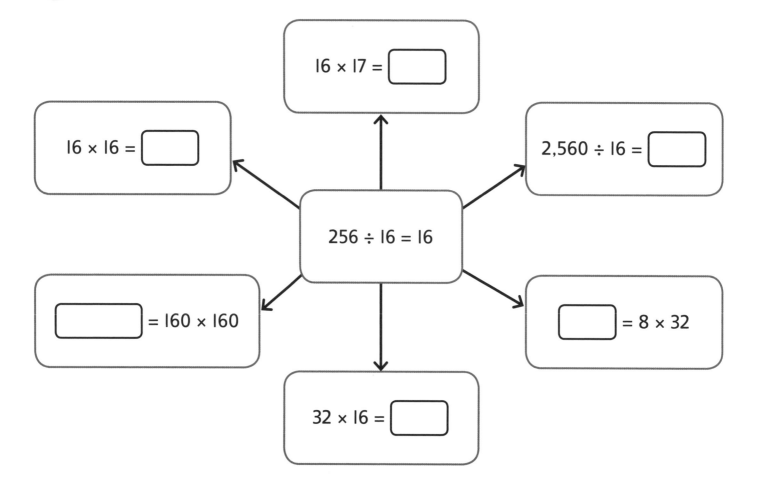

16 × 17 = ☐

16 × 16 = ☐

2,560 ÷ 16 = ☐

256 ÷ 16 = 16

☐ = 160 × 160

☐ = 8 × 32

32 × 16 = ☐

b) Add at least **three** more related facts of your own.

CHALLENGE

5 Find the missing digits. Write one digit in each box.

a) $\boxed{}\boxed{}\boxed{} \times \boxed{}1 = 2{,}761$

b) $\boxed{}\boxed{}^2 = 4{,}225$

You can use mental methods or make jottings in the space provided.

c) $\boxed{}\boxed{} \times 8\boxed{} = 2{,}025$

Reflect

Write three other facts you can work out from $85 \times 3 = 255$. Compare them with your partner. Have they got the same facts? Can you explain why they may be different?

→ **Textbook 6A p120**

End of unit check

My journal

① Olivia says 'I know that $3^2 = 9$, so 30^2 is 900.'

Mo says 'That means I can work out $29 \times 30 = 870$.'

Explain their reasoning. Are they both correct? Why or why not?

Power check

How do you feel about your work in this unit?

Power puzzle

'You can make any whole number by adding 2 or 3 prime numbers.'

Investigate the above statement. Is it true?

Use the chart below to help you begin your investigation.

4 = _____

5 = 2 + 3

6 = _____

7 = _____

8 = _____

9 = 3 + 3 + 3

10 = _____

11 = _____

12 = _____

13 = _____

14 = _____

15 = _____

16 = _____

17 = _____

18 = _____

19 = _____

20 = _____

100 = _____

101 = _____

200 = _____

Some numbers can be found by adding primes in different ways.
For example,
15 = 11 + 2 + 2
15 = 13 + 2
Challenge yourself to find out which numbers can be found in more than one way.

→ Textbook 6A p124

Simplifying fractions ①

① Write in the missing numbers to simplify the fractions.

a)

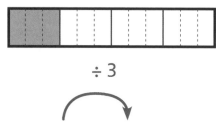

÷ 3

$$\frac{3}{12} = \frac{1}{\boxed{}}$$

÷ 3

b)

÷ 7

$$\frac{35}{42} = \frac{\boxed{}}{\boxed{}}$$

÷ $\boxed{}$

c)

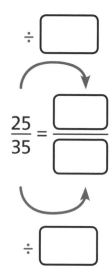

÷ $\boxed{}$

$$\frac{25}{35} = \frac{\boxed{}}{\boxed{}}$$

÷ $\boxed{}$

② Simplify these fractions.

a) $\dfrac{14}{24} = \dfrac{\boxed{}}{\boxed{}}$

b) $\dfrac{6}{15} = \dfrac{\boxed{}}{\boxed{}}$

c) $\dfrac{20}{45} = \dfrac{\boxed{}}{\boxed{}}$

d) $\dfrac{12}{16} = \dfrac{\boxed{}}{\boxed{}}$

e) $\dfrac{72}{\boxed{}} = \dfrac{9}{10}$

f) $\dfrac{\boxed{}}{24} = \dfrac{3}{4}$

③ Write in the missing numbers.

$$\frac{90}{120} = \frac{\boxed{}}{60} = \frac{15}{\boxed{}} = \frac{\boxed{}}{4}$$

4 Shade in the shapes to show the fractions.

a) 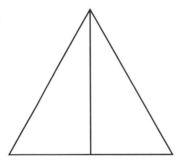 $\dfrac{10}{20}$

c) 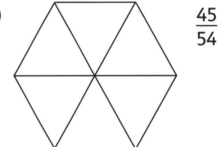 $\dfrac{20}{25}$

b) 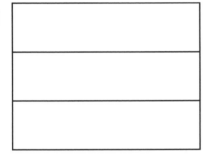 $\dfrac{6}{9}$

d) $\dfrac{45}{54}$

5 Ebo thinks $\dfrac{4}{6}$ in its simplest form is $\dfrac{1}{1\cdot5}$.

Is Ebo correct? Explain how you know.

_____

_____

_____

6 Circle the fraction that is **not** equivalent to the other fractions.

a) $\dfrac{5}{15}$ $\dfrac{15}{45}$ $\dfrac{10}{20}$ $\dfrac{20}{60}$

b) $\dfrac{12}{18}$ $\dfrac{120}{180}$ $\dfrac{18}{24}$ $\dfrac{24}{36}$

7 **a)** Which fraction can be simplified to $\frac{5}{8}$ and has a denominator of 40?

$$\frac{\boxed{}}{\boxed{}}$$

b) Which fraction can be simplified to $\frac{5}{8}$ and has a numerator of 40?

$$\frac{\boxed{}}{\boxed{}}$$

8 Calculate the missing values, simplifying if necessary.

a) $\dfrac{2 + \boxed{}}{3 + 12} = \dfrac{2}{3}$

c) $\dfrac{2 + 14}{3 + 17} = \dfrac{\boxed{}}{\boxed{}}$

b) $\dfrac{2 + 8}{3 + \boxed{}} = \dfrac{2}{5}$

d) $\dfrac{5 + \boxed{}}{3 + \boxed{}} = \dfrac{3}{4}$

Reflect

Explain how to simplify the fraction $\frac{12}{18}$.

_____

_____

_____

Simplifying fractions ❷

1 Simplify $4\frac{6}{10}$.

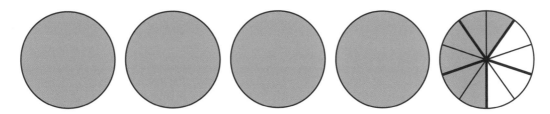

$\frac{6}{10} = \dfrac{\boxed{}}{\boxed{}}$

So $4\frac{6}{10} = 4\dfrac{\boxed{}}{\boxed{}}$

2 Simplify fully these fractions.

a) $\frac{16}{40} = \dfrac{\boxed{}}{\boxed{}}$

$1\frac{16}{40} = \boxed{}\dfrac{\boxed{}}{\boxed{}}$

$2\frac{16}{40} = \boxed{}\dfrac{\boxed{}}{\boxed{}}$

$32\frac{16}{40} = \boxed{}\dfrac{\boxed{}}{\boxed{}}$

b) $\frac{24}{40} = \dfrac{\boxed{}}{\boxed{}}$

$\frac{48}{80} = \dfrac{\boxed{}}{\boxed{}}$

$\frac{240}{400} = \dfrac{\boxed{}}{\boxed{}}$

$\frac{40}{24} = \dfrac{\boxed{}}{\boxed{}} = \boxed{}\dfrac{\boxed{}}{\boxed{}}$

What patterns did you notice?

In part a) I noticed _____ .

In part b) I noticed _____ .

3 Emma is trying to fully simplify some fractions.

Explain what mistake she has made in each question.

a) $\frac{6}{12} = \frac{3}{6}$ _____

_____

b) $\frac{10}{5} = \frac{1}{2}$ _____

_____

c) $8\frac{4}{10} = 4\frac{2}{5}$ _____

_____

4 Simplify each of the following fractions.

Write your answer as a mixed number where possible.

a) $6\frac{8}{12} =$

b) $\frac{30}{72} =$

c) $15\frac{24}{48} =$

d) $\frac{84}{132} =$

e) $\frac{40}{16} =$

f) $\frac{90}{72} =$

5 Which fraction is **not** equivalent to the other fractions?

$2\frac{12}{15}$ $\frac{28}{10}$ $\frac{42}{30}$

6 Which fraction does not simplify to a whole number?

$\dfrac{36}{6}$ $\dfrac{20}{40}$ $\dfrac{72}{36}$ $\dfrac{144}{36}$

7 Simplify these fractions.

CHALLENGE

a) $\dfrac{268}{64}$ b) $\dfrac{3352}{384}$

Remember to keep dividing the numerator and the denominator by the same number until you cannot simplify any more.

Reflect

Explain how to simplify $4\frac{16}{24}$.

→ Textbook 6A p132

Fractions on a number line

1 Write in the missing numbers.

a)

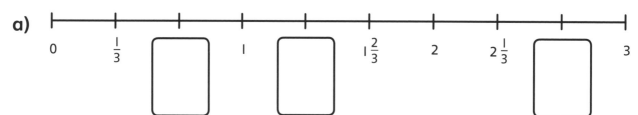

b)

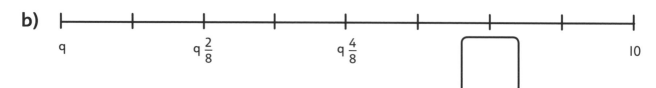

c)

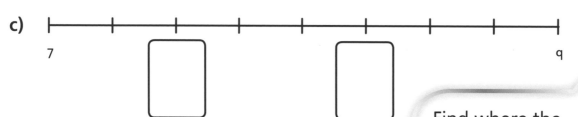

Find where the number 8 goes first.

2 Lee starts at $6\frac{2}{5}$.

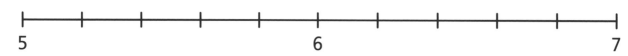

a) Lee counts back $\frac{3}{5}$. What number is Lee at now?

b) What is 1 less than $6\frac{2}{5}$?

3 Draw an arrow from each fraction to show its position on the number line.

a) $8\frac{2}{5}$ $9\frac{1}{5}$ $9\frac{1}{2}$

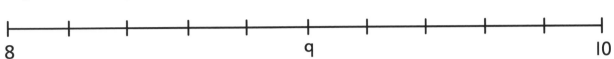

8   9   10

b) $\frac{17}{10}$ $1\frac{1}{5}$ $2\frac{9}{10}$ $\frac{30}{20}$

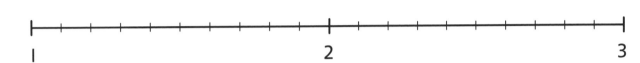

1   2   3

4 Use the number line to help you complete the patterns.

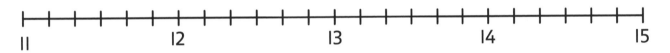

11   12   13   14   15

a) ⬚ , $13\frac{1}{6}$, $13\frac{4}{6}$, ⬚ , ⬚   c) ⬚ , ⬚ , $12\frac{5}{6}$, $12\frac{1}{6}$, ⬚

b) $11\frac{1}{2}$, $11\frac{5}{6}$, ⬚ , ⬚   d) ⬚ , $13\frac{1}{6}$, ⬚ , $11\frac{1}{6}$

5 Circle the pattern that does not go up or down by the same amount each time.

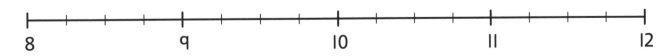

8   9   10   11   12

a) $8, 8\frac{1}{2}, 9, 9\frac{1}{2}$ c) $9\frac{3}{4}, 10\frac{1}{2}, 11\frac{1}{4}, 12$

b) $11\frac{1}{4}, 10\frac{3}{4}, 10\frac{2}{8}, 9\frac{3}{4}$ d) $9\frac{1}{4}, 10, 10\frac{3}{4}, 11\frac{1}{4}$

6 Place these numbers onto both number lines.

$7\frac{1}{8}$ $5\frac{1}{2}$ $9\frac{3}{4}$ $7\frac{5}{10}$

a)

0   10

b)

5   10

What do you notice about the distances between the numbers on each number line?

_____

_____

_____

_____

Reflect

What numbers are the arrows pointing to? How do you know?

_____

_____

_____

Comparing and ordering fractions ❶

1 **a)** Compare the fractions $\frac{1}{2}$ and $\frac{3}{4}$.

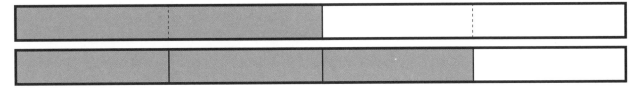

The LCM of 2 and 4 is ☐.

$\frac{1}{2} = \dfrac{\boxed{}}{4}$

So $\frac{1}{2}$ ◯ $\frac{3}{4}$.

b) Compare the fractions $\frac{3}{5}$ and $\frac{7}{10}$.

The LCM of 5 and 10 is ☐.

$\frac{3}{5} = \dfrac{\boxed{}}{\boxed{}}$

So $\frac{3}{5}$ ◯ $\frac{7}{10}$.

c) Compare the fractions $\frac{3}{8}$ and $\frac{2}{3}$. The LCM of 8 and ☐ is ☐.

$\frac{3}{8} = \dfrac{\boxed{}}{\boxed{}}$

$\frac{2}{3} = \dfrac{\boxed{}}{\boxed{}}$

So $\frac{3}{8}$ ◯ $\frac{2}{3}$.

d) Compare the fractions $\frac{3}{5}$ and $\frac{4}{7}$. The LCM of ☐ and ☐ is ☐.

$\frac{3}{5} = \dfrac{\boxed{}}{\boxed{}}$

$\frac{4}{7} = \dfrac{\boxed{}}{\boxed{}}$

So $\frac{3}{5}$ ◯ $\frac{4}{7}$.

2 Here are some fractions.

$$\frac{4}{5} \qquad \frac{7}{10} \qquad \frac{3}{4}$$

a) What is the LCM of 5, 10 and 4? Explain how you know.

b) Which is the biggest fraction? How do you know?

3 A fraction of each shape is shaded.

A   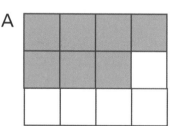   B   C   D   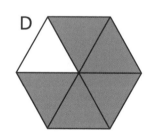

Put the shapes in order of the fraction shaded. Start with the shape with the biggest fraction shaded.

4 Put these fractions in order from biggest to smallest.

a) $\frac{11}{15}, \frac{2}{3}, \frac{7}{10}, \frac{1}{2}$ **b)** $\frac{1}{6}, \frac{3}{3}, \frac{7}{8}, \frac{3}{4}$

5 Here is a school newspaper article.

Y6 children at Power Maths Primary voted on their favourite flavour of ice-cream. $\frac{3}{8}$ of the children chose strawberry. $\frac{2}{5}$ of the children chose chocolate. $\frac{9}{40}$ of the children chose lemon flavour. This shows that lemon is the most popular flavour.

Do you agree with the article? Why?

_____

_____

6 Write in the missing digits so that the fractions are in ascending order.

a) $\frac{1}{3}$ $\frac{\boxed{}}{12}$ $\frac{2}{3}$ $\frac{5}{6}$

Remember that ascending means from smallest to biggest.

b) $\frac{\boxed{}}{2}$ $\frac{7}{\boxed{}}$ $\frac{\boxed{}}{3}$ $\frac{\boxed{}}{8}$

Reflect

Lexi says '$\frac{5}{8}$ is less than $\frac{5}{12}$ because 8 is less than 12.' Is Lexi correct?

_____

_____

_____

→ Textbook 6A p140

Comparing and ordering fractions ❷

 1   **a)** Compare the fractions $4\frac{2}{3}$ and $4\frac{1}{2}$.

$4\frac{2}{3} = 4\dfrac{\boxed{}}{6}$ $\qquad$ $4\frac{1}{2} = 4\dfrac{\boxed{}}{6}$ $\qquad$ So $4\frac{2}{3} \bigcirc 4\frac{1}{2}$.

b) Compare the fractions $\frac{11}{4}$ and $\frac{19}{8}$.

$\dfrac{11}{4} = \dfrac{\boxed{}}{\boxed{}}$ $\qquad$ So $\dfrac{11}{4} \bigcirc \dfrac{19}{8}$.

c) Compare the fractions $2\frac{1}{5}$ and $2\frac{1}{3}$.

The LCM of 5 and 3 is $\boxed{}$.

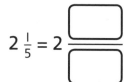 $2\frac{1}{5} = 2\dfrac{\boxed{}}{\boxed{}}$ $\qquad$ $2\frac{1}{3} = 2\dfrac{\boxed{}}{\boxed{}}$ $\qquad$ So $2\frac{1}{5} \bigcirc 2\frac{1}{3}$.

2   **a)** Explain how you would compare $3\frac{3}{8}$ and $\frac{29}{8}$.

_____

_____

_____

b) Which is bigger, $5\frac{1}{6}$ or $4\frac{5}{6}$? How do you know?

_____

_____

_____

3 **a)** Compare the fractions $8\frac{2}{3}$ and $\frac{60}{7}$.

The LCM of 3 and 7 is ☐ .

$$8\frac{2}{3} = 8\frac{\boxed{}}{\boxed{}} \qquad \frac{60}{7} = \boxed{}\frac{\boxed{}}{7}$$

$$= \boxed{}\frac{\boxed{}}{\boxed{}} \qquad \text{So } 8\frac{2}{3}\bigcirc\frac{60}{7}.$$

b) Compare the fractions $\frac{11}{7}$ and $1\frac{11}{14}$.

c) Compare the fractions $\frac{35}{6}$ and $\frac{45}{8}$.

4 Put these fractions in ascending order:

$\frac{87}{10}$, $\frac{27}{3}$, $8\frac{7}{15}$, $\frac{17}{2}$

5 Which fraction is closest to 4?

$4\frac{1}{4}$, $4\frac{1}{5}$, $4\frac{3}{10}$

6 Three fractions are placed on a number line.

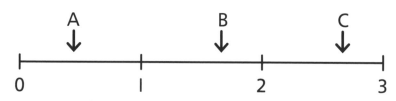

The denominators and numerators have all been mixed up.

Work out the fractions A, B and C using the number cards.

A = ⬚/⬚   B = ⬚/⬚   C = ⬚/⬚

| 3 | 6 | 9 |
| 4 | 8 | 10 |

Reflect

Explain how to compare $2\frac{2}{5}$ and $\frac{11}{4}$.

→ **Textbook 6A p144**

Adding and subtracting fractions ❶

1 **a)** Work out $\frac{3}{4} + \frac{1}{10}$.

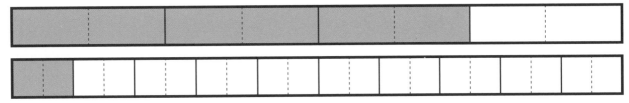

The LCM of 4 and 10 is ☐ .

$\frac{3}{4} = \frac{\boxed{}}{\boxed{}}$ $\frac{1}{10} = \frac{\boxed{}}{\boxed{}}$ $\frac{\boxed{}}{\boxed{}} + \frac{\boxed{}}{\boxed{}} = \frac{\boxed{}}{\boxed{}}$

So $\frac{3}{4} + \frac{1}{10} = \frac{\boxed{}}{\boxed{}}$

b) Work out $\frac{7}{8} - \frac{5}{12}$.

The LCM of ☐ and ☐ is ☐ .

$\frac{7}{8} = \frac{\boxed{}}{\boxed{}}$ $\frac{5}{12} = \frac{\boxed{}}{\boxed{}}$ $\frac{\boxed{}}{\boxed{}} - \frac{\boxed{}}{\boxed{}} = \frac{\boxed{}}{\boxed{}}$

So $\frac{7}{8} - \frac{5}{12} = \frac{\boxed{}}{\boxed{}}$

2 $\frac{3}{4}$ of a metre is cut off this ribbon.
What length of ribbon remains?

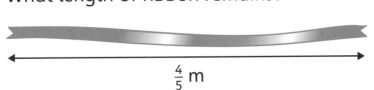

$\frac{4}{5}$ m

3 What mistake has Ambika made when adding the two fractions? Explain the correct way to complete the problem.

$\frac{3}{10} + \frac{1}{5} = \frac{4}{15}$

_____

_____

4 Complete these additions and subtractions.

a) $\frac{2}{5} + \frac{7}{15} =$

c) $\frac{3}{4} - \frac{2}{3} =$

b) $\frac{5}{8} + \frac{1}{3} =$

d) $\frac{9}{10} - \frac{1}{4} =$

5 Andy thinks of a fraction.

He subtracts $\frac{2}{3}$ from it and his answer is $\frac{4}{21}$.

What fraction was he thinking of?

I wrote it out like this

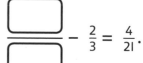

$\boxed{} - \frac{2}{3} = \frac{4}{21}.$

Then I thought about what I needed to do with $\frac{4}{21}$ and $\frac{2}{3}$.

6 Ebo reads $\frac{5}{9}$ of a book at school. He reads $\frac{2}{5}$ of the book at home.

Richard says, 'You must have read all of the book.'

Is Richard correct? Explain how you know.

_____

_____

_____

7 Fill in the missing numbers to make the calculations correct.

a)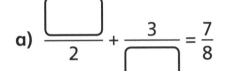

b)

Reflect

Amelia is working out the answer to $\frac{2}{5} + \frac{1}{4}$.

Amelia works out $\frac{2}{20} + \frac{1}{20} = \frac{3}{20}$. Explain the mistake Amelia has made and correct her.

_____

_____

_____

→ Textbook 6A p148

Adding and subtracting fractions ❷

1 **a)** Work out $4\frac{2}{3} + 1\frac{1}{6}$.

Add the wholes: $4 + 1 = \boxed{}$

Add the parts: $\frac{2}{3} = \dfrac{\boxed{}}{6}$

$\frac{2}{3} + \frac{1}{6} = \dfrac{\boxed{}}{6} + \frac{1}{6} = \dfrac{\boxed{}}{\boxed{}}$

So $4\frac{2}{3} + 1\frac{1}{6} = \boxed{}\ \dfrac{\boxed{}}{\boxed{}}$

b) Work out $3\frac{3}{4} - 1\frac{1}{6}$.

Subtract the wholes: $\boxed{} - \boxed{} = \boxed{}$

Subtract the parts: $\frac{3}{4} = \dfrac{\boxed{}}{\boxed{}}$ $\qquad \frac{1}{6} = \dfrac{\boxed{}}{\boxed{}}$

$\frac{3}{4} - \frac{1}{6} = \dfrac{\boxed{}}{\boxed{}} - \dfrac{\boxed{}}{\boxed{}} = \dfrac{\boxed{}}{\boxed{}}$

So $3\frac{3}{4} - 1\frac{1}{6} = \boxed{}\ \dfrac{\boxed{}}{\boxed{}}$

> Remember you need to find the lowest common multiple of 4 and 6. Think of the first number in the 4 and 6 times-tables.

2 Work out these additions and subtractions.

a) $2\frac{2}{5} + 1\frac{1}{3}$

c) $3\frac{7}{10} + 1\frac{1}{4}$

b) $3\frac{4}{9} + 2\frac{1}{3}$

d) $8\frac{3}{4} - \frac{3}{5}$

3 A bucket contains $12\frac{1}{2}$ litres of water. There is a hole in the bucket.

Each minute $1\frac{1}{5}$ litres of water leak out of the bucket.

a) How much water will leak out in 2 minutes?

b) How much water is left in the bucket after 2 minutes?

4 Reena has three fraction cards. She adds two of the cards together. What is the biggest possible number she could make?

$11\frac{2}{3}$ $3\frac{2}{9}$ $3\frac{1}{4}$

5 Jamie thinks of two numbers and adds them together.

CHALLENGE

Her answer is $21\frac{4}{5}$. One of the numbers Jamie thinks of is $16\frac{3}{8}$.

What is the other number? How can you check your answer?

Reflect

Ebo is working out the missing part. Ebo says you need to add the two fractions. Is Ebo correct? Explain your answer.

$7\frac{5}{6}$	
?	$5\frac{3}{4}$

Adding fractions

1 **a)** Work out $3\frac{2}{3} + 2\frac{3}{4}$.

Show your method.

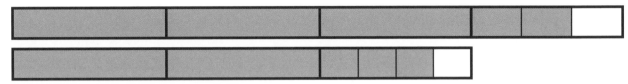

b) Work out $\frac{5}{6} + 1\frac{1}{2}$.

2 Work out these additions.

a) $8\frac{2}{3} + \frac{9}{10}$

b) $2\frac{4}{14} + 5\frac{5}{7}$

3 Kate wants to add $12\frac{3}{5}$ and $7\frac{3}{4}$.

She changes each number to an improper fraction.

Is this the most efficient method? Explain your answer.

4 Zac spends $3\frac{1}{4}$ hours on his homework in a week.

Aki spends $\frac{5}{6}$ hours more.

How many hours does Aki spend on his homework?

5 What is the distance from the café to the beach?

café $1\frac{1}{2}$ km

beach $3\frac{3}{5}$ km

6 Mo wants to put a fence around the edge of his rectangular garden.

His garden is $3\frac{3}{4}$ metres wide and $5\frac{7}{10}$ metres long.

Fencing comes in packs of 4 metres.

How many packs does Mo need to buy?

Reflect

Explain how to work out $4\frac{5}{6} + 2\frac{3}{8}$.

→ **Textbook 6A p156**

Subtracting fractions

Use whichever method you feel happier with.

1 Work out these subtractions, showing your working.

a) $3\frac{1}{4} - 1\frac{1}{2}$

c) $12\frac{1}{6} - 5\frac{1}{4}$

b) $4\frac{1}{3} - 3\frac{3}{5}$

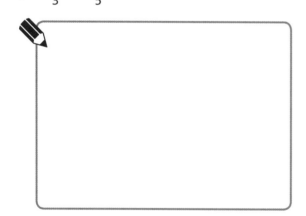

d) $5\frac{3}{4} - \frac{9}{10}$

2 Work out these subtractions.

a) $5\frac{3}{5} - 2$

b) $5 - 2\frac{3}{5}$

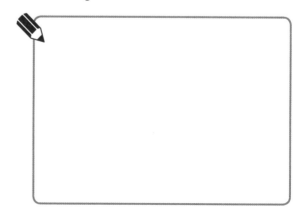

3 Complete the part-whole model.

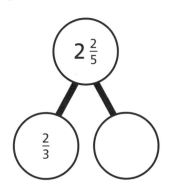

4 How tall is the baby giraffe?

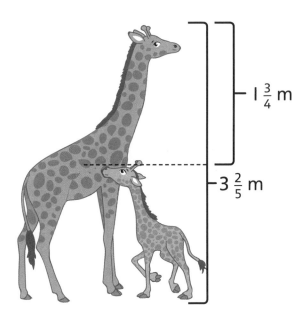

$1\frac{3}{4}$ m

$3\frac{2}{5}$ m

5 Use the number line to work out $3\frac{1}{5} - 1\frac{5}{6}$.

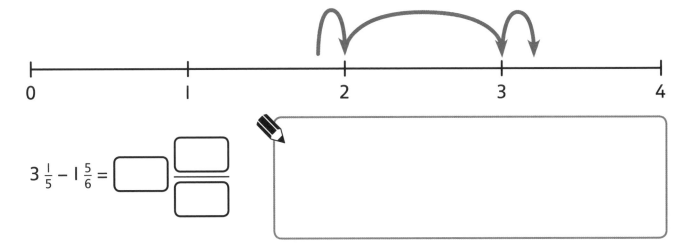

$3\frac{1}{5} - 1\frac{5}{6} =$ ☐ ☐/☐

6 Subtract  from .

7 $\bigstar + 3\frac{5}{6} = 5\frac{3}{4}$

$6\frac{1}{3} - \bigstar = \heartsuit$

Work out the value of $\heartsuit$ showing your working.

 CHALLENGE

Reflect

Explain how to work out $5\frac{1}{5} - 2\frac{3}{4}$. Did you use the same method as your partner?

Problem solving – adding and subtracting fractions ❶

1 Olivia weighs two pieces of fruit.

What is the total mass of the apple and pineapple?

2 Calculate the perimeter of the isosceles triangle.

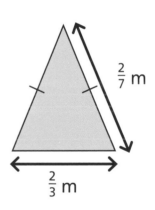

$\frac{2}{7}$ m

$\frac{2}{3}$ m

Perimeter means the distance around the shape.

3 Toshi saws off $1\frac{1}{2}$ metres of wood. How much wood remains?

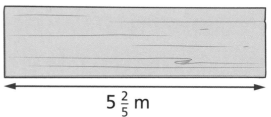

$5\frac{2}{5}$ m

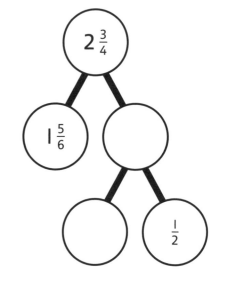

4 Complete the part-whole model.

$2\frac{3}{4}$

$1\frac{5}{6}$

$\frac{1}{2}$

5 What is the total length of the pencils?

$8\frac{3}{5}$ cm $13\frac{3}{4}$ cm

CHALLENGE

6 Baby Anna weighs $\frac{2}{3}$ lbs less than baby Evie.

Georgia weighs $\frac{3}{5}$ lbs more than Evie.

How much more does Georgia weigh than Anna?

Anna	Georgia	Evie
		$8\frac{1}{2}$ lbs

Reflect

Write an addition or subtraction problem that has $2\frac{1}{3}$ as the answer.

→ **Textbook 6A p164**

Problem solving – adding and subtracting fractions ❷

1 Calculate the height of the tallest elephant.

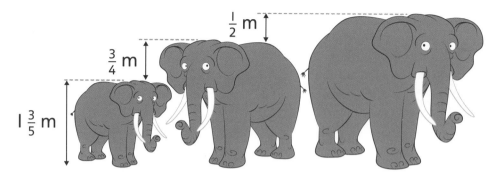

2 A picnic basket contains a melon and a bottle of water.

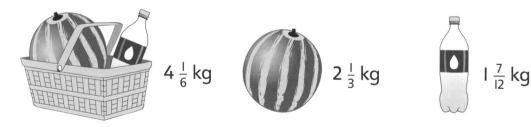

$4\frac{1}{6}$ kg $2\frac{1}{3}$ kg $1\frac{7}{12}$ kg

What is the mass of the empty picnic basket?

3 A pop star's new single has $5\frac{1}{2}$ million downloads on Friday.

On Saturday there are $\frac{3}{4}$ million more downloads than on Friday.

How many downloads were there in total on Friday and Saturday?

4 A spider is climbing up a drainpipe 6 metres high.

The spider climbs $3\frac{1}{5}$ metres up the drainpipe, then stops for a rest.

During its rest, the spider slides down $\frac{2}{3}$ metres.

The spider then climbs another $2\frac{7}{10}$ metres up the drainpipe.

There is a lot to do in this question. Try to answer the question one step at a time.

How many metres from the top of the pipe is the spider now?

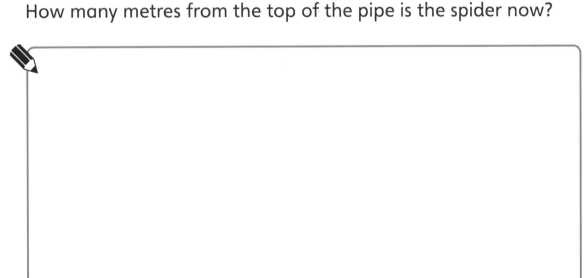

5 How much bigger is the distance BC than the distance AB?

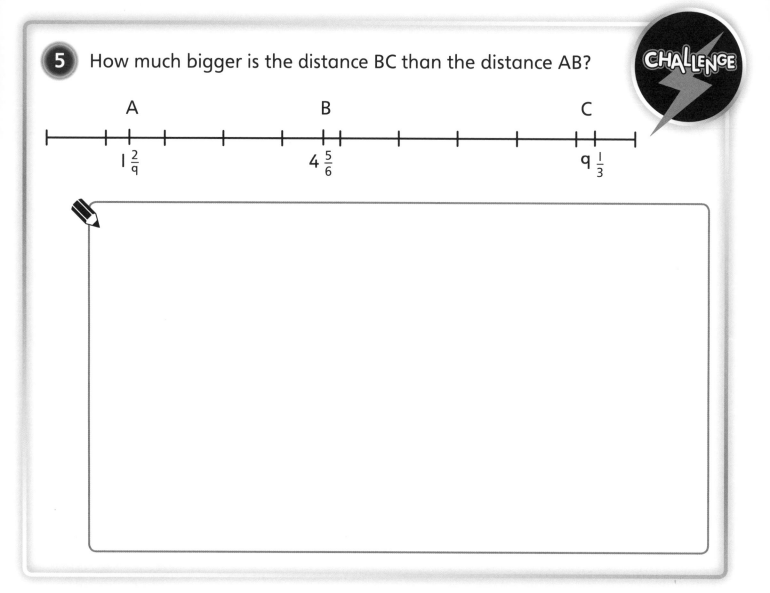

A   B   C

$1\frac{2}{9}$ $4\frac{5}{6}$ $9\frac{1}{3}$

Reflect

Did you find a question difficult? Which one? What mistake did you make?
What about your partners – did they find any questions difficult? Compare with
a partner to see which question they found difficult.

End of unit check

My journal

1 Here are six calculations from the lessons.

A $\frac{2}{3} + \frac{4}{5}$	C $2\frac{3}{8} - 1\frac{1}{3}$	E $3\frac{1}{2} + 1\frac{8}{9}$
B $\frac{7}{10} + \frac{1}{4}$	D $3\frac{2}{5} + 4\frac{3}{4}$	F $\frac{1}{3} + \frac{1}{2} + \frac{1}{4}$

Have a go at each question, showing your working.

Put the letters into the table below to show how difficult you found each question.

I solved this quite easily. I did not need help.	I had to look back through my book. I needed a bit of help and then I was fine.	I forgot how to answer this question or I needed a lot of help.

2 Jamie and Danny are working out $5\frac{1}{4} - 3\frac{2}{5}$.

I am going to convert the mixed numbers into improper fractions with a common denominator and then subtract the fractions.

I am going to subtract the wholes and then the fractions, using equivalent fractions with a common denominator. I think I need to do something to $5\frac{1}{4}$ first though.

Danny

Jamie

Whose method is correct? What should the answer be?

Power check

How do you feel about your work in this unit?

Power puzzle

1 Here are two number puzzles.

a)

| 2 | 3 | 4 | 5 | 6 | 7 |

Place the digits in the calculation. Use each digit once only.

Where do the numbers go? Explain your reasoning.

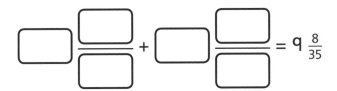

$$\boxed{}\,\frac{\boxed{}}{\boxed{}} + \boxed{}\,\frac{\boxed{}}{\boxed{}} = 9\frac{8}{35}$$

b) All the rows and columns add up to the same number.

Work out the missing values.

$1\frac{3}{10}$	$2\frac{1}{2}$	$3\frac{1}{5}$
$4\frac{3}{4}$		
	$3\frac{5}{6}$	

> You can add or subtract to find the missing values. Whichever you did, now use the inverse operation to check your answers.

→ Textbook 6A p172

Multiplying a fraction by a whole number

1 **a)** Work out $\frac{1}{4} \times 7$.

$\frac{1}{4} \times 7 = \dfrac{\boxed{}}{\boxed{}} = \boxed{}\dfrac{\boxed{}}{\boxed{}}$

b) Work out $\frac{2}{5} \times 4$.

$\frac{2}{5} \times 4 = \dfrac{\boxed{}}{\boxed{}} = \boxed{}\dfrac{\boxed{}}{\boxed{}}$

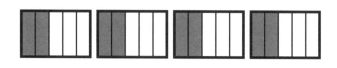

c) Work out $\frac{2}{3} \times 6$.

$\frac{2}{3} \times 6 = \dfrac{\boxed{}}{\boxed{}} = \boxed{}$

2 Work out these multiplications.

a) $\frac{1}{2} \times 7 = \dfrac{\boxed{}}{\boxed{}} = \boxed{}\dfrac{\boxed{}}{\boxed{}}$

b) $\frac{4}{5} \times 3 = \dfrac{\boxed{}}{\boxed{}} = \boxed{}\dfrac{\boxed{}}{\boxed{}}$

c) $\frac{3}{8} \times 6 = \dfrac{\boxed{}}{\boxed{}} = \boxed{}\dfrac{\boxed{}}{\boxed{}}$

d) $\frac{7}{10} \times 5 = \dfrac{\boxed{}}{\boxed{}} = \boxed{}\dfrac{\boxed{}}{\boxed{}}$

3 Work out $1\frac{3}{5} \times 3$ in two different ways.

  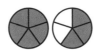

$1 \times 3 = \boxed{}$ and $1\frac{3}{5} = \dfrac{\boxed{}}{5}$

$\dfrac{3}{5} \times 3 = \dfrac{\boxed{}}{\boxed{}} = \boxed{}\dfrac{\boxed{}}{\boxed{}}$

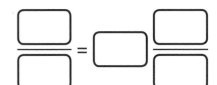

$\boxed{} + \boxed{}\dfrac{\boxed{}}{\boxed{}} = \boxed{}\dfrac{\boxed{}}{\boxed{}}$

So $1\frac{3}{5} \times 3 = \boxed{}\dfrac{\boxed{}}{\boxed{}}$.

4 Work out these multiplications.

a) $\frac{11}{5} \times 6$

b) $2\frac{1}{3} \times 8$

c) $2\frac{3}{4} \times 3$

d) $6 \times 3\frac{2}{5}$

5 Kate says $\frac{2}{3} \times 4 = \frac{8}{12}$. What mistake has Kate made?

_____

_____

6 Rusty the dog eats $\frac{1}{5}$ of a bag of dog biscuits each day.

How many bags does his owner need to buy to feed him for 11 days?

7 **a)** A double decker bus is $18\frac{3}{5}$ metres long.
What is the total length of 12 double decker buses?

CHALLENGE

b) Work out the missing numbers.

$$\frac{1}{5} \times \boxed{} = \frac{4}{5}$$

$$\frac{\boxed{}}{7} \times 5 = \frac{10}{7}$$

$$\frac{2}{3} \times \boxed{} = 3\frac{1}{3}$$

$$\frac{3}{5} \times \boxed{} = \frac{12}{5}$$

$$\frac{\boxed{}}{7} \times 3 = \frac{15}{7}$$

$$\frac{2}{3} \times \boxed{} = 6$$

Reflect

Explain why $1\frac{2}{3} \times 4$ is equal to $6\frac{2}{3}$.

Multiplying a fraction by a fraction

1 Zac is baking cookies.

a) The bag of flour is $\frac{1}{4}$ full. He uses $\frac{1}{2}$ of the flour in the bag.

What fraction of the whole bag does Zac use?

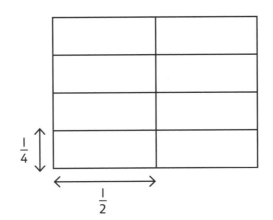

$$\frac{1}{2} \times \frac{1}{4} = \frac{\boxed{}}{\boxed{}}$$

Zac uses $\dfrac{\boxed{}}{\boxed{}}$ of the bag of flour.

b) The bag of chocolate chips is $\frac{1}{2}$ full.

Zac needs $\frac{3}{4}$ of the chocolate chips.

What fraction of the whole bag does he need?

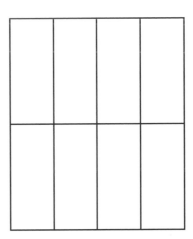

$$\frac{\boxed{}}{\boxed{}} \times \frac{\boxed{}}{\boxed{}} = \frac{\boxed{}}{\boxed{}}$$

Zac needs $\dfrac{\boxed{}}{\boxed{}}$ of the bag.

2 **a)** Complete the diagram to work out $\frac{1}{5} \times \frac{1}{3}$.

$$\frac{1}{5} \times \frac{1}{3} = \frac{\boxed{}}{\boxed{}}$$

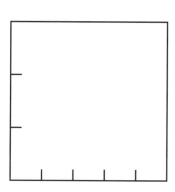

b) Complete the diagram to work out $\frac{2}{3}$ of $\frac{2}{5}$.

$$\frac{\boxed{}}{\boxed{}} \times \frac{\boxed{}}{\boxed{}} = \frac{\boxed{}}{\boxed{}}$$

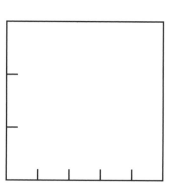

3 Draw diagrams to help you work out these calculations. Give each answer in its simplest form.

a) $\frac{3}{4} \times \frac{2}{5} = \frac{\boxed{}}{\boxed{}}$

b) $\frac{2}{3}$ of $\frac{5}{6} = \frac{\boxed{}}{\boxed{}}$

4 These diagrams show the result of two fractions being multiplied together. What could the questions have been?

a)
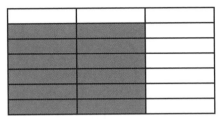

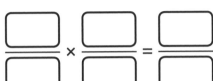

b)

5 Is this statement always true, sometimes true or never true? Explain your answer.

CHALLENGE

'When you multiply a proper fraction by another proper fraction, the answer will be smaller than the two original fractions.'

The statement is_____ because_____

_____

_____

A proper fraction has a numerator that is less than the denominator.

Reflect

Draw a diagram to show why $\frac{1}{2} \times \frac{3}{5} = \frac{3}{10}$.

Multiplying a fraction by a fraction ②

1

a) Use the diagram to work out $\frac{3}{4} \times \frac{1}{2}$.

$$\frac{3}{4} \times \frac{1}{2} = \frac{\boxed{}}{\boxed{}}$$

b) Reena says you can work out the answer without drawing a diagram. Explain how.

_____

_____

2 Work out these calculations without using a diagram.

a) $\dfrac{2}{9} \times \dfrac{1}{4} = \dfrac{\boxed{} \times \boxed{}}{\boxed{} \times \boxed{}} = \dfrac{\boxed{}}{\boxed{}} = \dfrac{\boxed{}}{\boxed{}}$

b) $\dfrac{2}{9} \times \dfrac{3}{4} = \dfrac{\boxed{} \times \boxed{}}{\boxed{} \times \boxed{}} = \dfrac{\boxed{}}{\boxed{}} = \dfrac{\boxed{}}{\boxed{}}$

c) $\dfrac{1}{5} \times \dfrac{10}{11} = \dfrac{\boxed{} \times \boxed{}}{\boxed{} \times \boxed{}} = \dfrac{\boxed{}}{\boxed{}} = \dfrac{\boxed{}}{\boxed{}}$

3 Work out these calculations.

a) $\dfrac{1}{4} \times \dfrac{1}{3} = \dfrac{\boxed{}}{\boxed{}}$

b) $\dfrac{3}{4} \times \dfrac{1}{7} = \dfrac{\boxed{}}{\boxed{}}$

c) $\dfrac{\boxed{}}{\boxed{}} = \dfrac{2}{3} \times \dfrac{2}{5}$

d) $\dfrac{1}{2}$ of $\dfrac{7}{8} = \dfrac{\boxed{}}{\boxed{}}$

e) $\dfrac{\boxed{}}{\boxed{}} = \dfrac{5}{6}$ of $\dfrac{7}{8}$

f) $\dfrac{7}{23} \times \dfrac{9}{10} = \dfrac{\boxed{}}{\boxed{}}$

4 Fill in the boxes to complete the calculations.

a) $\dfrac{\boxed{}}{3} \times \dfrac{2}{\boxed{}} = \dfrac{2}{15}$

c) $\dfrac{\boxed{}}{5} \times \dfrac{1}{\boxed{}} \times \dfrac{3}{7} = \dfrac{9}{70}$

b) $\dfrac{\boxed{}}{3} \times \dfrac{\boxed{}}{6} = \dfrac{5}{18}$

d) $\dfrac{7}{12} \times \dfrac{1}{\boxed{}} = \dfrac{1}{6} \times \dfrac{\boxed{}}{6}$

5 Aki and Kate are working out $\frac{2}{7} \times \frac{3}{8}$.

I think the answer is $\frac{5}{56}$.

Aki

No, the answer is $\frac{3}{28}$.

Kate

a) What mistake has Aki made?

_____

_____

b) Has Kate got the correct answer? Explain how you know.

_____

_____

133

6 Use fractions to complete the number sentences.
Find two different ways to get each answer.

CHALLENGE

a) $\dfrac{\boxed{}}{\boxed{}} \times \dfrac{\boxed{}}{\boxed{}} = \dfrac{8}{15}$
$\dfrac{\boxed{}}{\boxed{}} \times \dfrac{\boxed{}}{\boxed{}} = \dfrac{8}{15}$

b) $\dfrac{\boxed{}}{\boxed{}} \times \dfrac{\boxed{}}{\boxed{}} = \dfrac{12}{21}$
$\dfrac{\boxed{}}{\boxed{}} \times \dfrac{\boxed{}}{\boxed{}} = \dfrac{12}{21}$

c) $\dfrac{\boxed{}}{\boxed{}} \times \dfrac{\boxed{}}{\boxed{}} = \dfrac{1}{2}$
$\dfrac{\boxed{}}{\boxed{}} \times \dfrac{\boxed{}}{\boxed{}} = \dfrac{1}{2}$

d) $\dfrac{\boxed{}}{\boxed{}} \times \dfrac{\boxed{}}{\boxed{}} \times \dfrac{\boxed{}}{\boxed{}} = \dfrac{9}{48}$
$\dfrac{\boxed{}}{\boxed{}} \times \dfrac{\boxed{}}{\boxed{}} \times \dfrac{\boxed{}}{\boxed{}} = \dfrac{9}{48}$

Reflect

Describe what you do when you multiply two fractions together.
Compare your method with your partner's method. Is it the same or different?

_____

_____

_____

Dividing a fraction by a whole number

1 **a)** A circle is divided into 6 equal parts.

Follow these instructions:

- Divide 1 of the sixths into 2 parts.

- Shade in 1 of the parts you have just made.

What fraction of the circle is shaded?

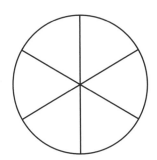

$\frac{1}{6} \div 2 = \dfrac{\boxed{}}{\boxed{}}$

$\dfrac{\boxed{}}{\boxed{}}$ of the circle is shaded.

b) Use the diagram to work out $\frac{1}{5} \div 2$.

$\frac{1}{5} \div 2 = \dfrac{\boxed{}}{\boxed{}}$

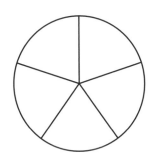

2 Use the diagram to show $\frac{1}{8} \div 2$.

$\frac{1}{8} \div 2 = \dfrac{\boxed{}}{\boxed{}}$

135

3 Use the diagrams to work out these divisions.

a) $\dfrac{1}{4} \div 3 = \dfrac{\boxed{}}{\boxed{}}$

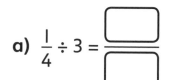

b) $\dfrac{1}{3} \div 4 = \dfrac{\boxed{}}{\boxed{}}$

4 Write the calculations to match these diagrams.

a) $\dfrac{\boxed{}}{\boxed{}} \div \boxed{} = \dfrac{\boxed{}}{\boxed{}}$

b) $\dfrac{\boxed{}}{\boxed{}} \div \boxed{} = \dfrac{\boxed{}}{\boxed{}}$

c) $\dfrac{\boxed{}}{\boxed{}} \div \boxed{} = \dfrac{\boxed{}}{\boxed{}}$

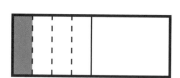

5 Find the missing numbers and fractions.

a) $\dfrac{1}{9} \div 2 = \dfrac{\boxed{}}{\boxed{}}$

d) $\dfrac{1}{4} \div 5 = \dfrac{\boxed{}}{\boxed{}}$

g) $\dfrac{1}{4} \div \boxed{} = \dfrac{1}{8}$

b) $\dfrac{1}{3} \div 6 = \dfrac{\boxed{}}{\boxed{}}$

e) $\dfrac{\boxed{}}{\boxed{}} = \dfrac{1}{7} \div 4$

h) $\dfrac{1}{10} \div \boxed{} = \dfrac{1}{30}$

c) $\dfrac{1}{10} \div 3 = \dfrac{\boxed{}}{\boxed{}}$

f) $\dfrac{1}{6} \div 4 = \dfrac{\boxed{}}{\boxed{}}$

i) $\dfrac{1}{\boxed{}} \div 3 = \dfrac{1}{9}$

6 **a)** Kate shares $\frac{1}{3}$ of a pizza equally between her and her two friends.

What fraction of the whole pizza does each person get?

Each person gets $\frac{\boxed{}}{\boxed{}}$ of the pizza.

b) Emma has a chocolate bar. She eats $\frac{5}{6}$ of the bar.

She shares the remainder equally with Max.

What fraction of the whole bar does Max get?

Max gets $\frac{\boxed{}}{\boxed{}}$ of the bar.

7 Find six different ways to make the calculation correct.

CHALLENGE

$\frac{1}{\boxed{}} \div \boxed{} = \frac{1}{48}$ $\frac{1}{\boxed{}} \div \boxed{} = \frac{1}{48}$ $\frac{1}{\boxed{}} \div \boxed{} = \frac{1}{48}$

$\frac{1}{\boxed{}} \div \boxed{} = \frac{1}{48}$ $\frac{1}{\boxed{}} \div \boxed{} = \frac{1}{48}$ $\frac{1}{\boxed{}} \div \boxed{} = \frac{1}{48}$

Reflect

$\frac{1}{10} \div 2 = \frac{1}{5}$ Is this true or false? Explain your reasoning.

→ Textbook 6A p188

Dividing a fraction by a whole number ❷

1 This circle is divided into twelfths.

4 of the twelfths can be divided into 2 equal groups.

How many twelfths are there in each group?

There are ☐ twelfths in each group.

Write this as a division.

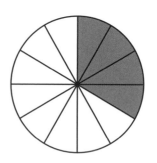

$$\frac{4}{12} \div 2 = \frac{\boxed{}}{\boxed{}}$$

2 Use the diagrams to help you work out the divisions.

a)

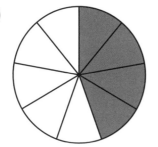

$$\frac{4}{9} \div 2 = \frac{\boxed{}}{\boxed{}}$$

b)

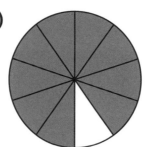

$$\frac{9}{10} \div 3 = \frac{\boxed{}}{\boxed{}}$$

c)

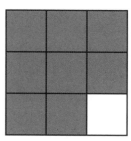

$$\frac{8}{9} \div 2 = \frac{\boxed{}}{\boxed{}}$$

3 Work out these divisions.

a) $\frac{10}{11} \div 5 = \frac{\boxed{}}{\boxed{}}$

b) $\frac{4}{5} \div 4 = \frac{\boxed{}}{\boxed{}}$

4 Write a calculation for this diagram.

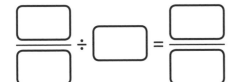 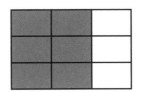

5 Work out these divisions.

a) $\dfrac{5}{9} \div 5 = \dfrac{\Box}{\Box}$

c) $\dfrac{6}{7} \div 2 = \dfrac{\Box}{\Box}$

b) $\dfrac{3}{4} \div 3 = \dfrac{\Box}{\Box}$

d) $\dfrac{8}{15} \div 2 = \dfrac{\Box}{\Box}$

6 Complete these number sentences.

a) $\dfrac{\Box}{5} \div 2 = \dfrac{1}{5}$

$\dfrac{\Box}{5} \div 2 = \dfrac{2}{5}$

b) $\dfrac{\Box}{20} \div 3 = \dfrac{2}{20}$

$\dfrac{\Box}{20} \div 3 = \dfrac{5}{20}$

c) $\dfrac{14}{15} \div \Box = \dfrac{2}{15}$

$\dfrac{14}{15} \div \Box = \dfrac{7}{15}$

$\dfrac{14}{15} \div \Box = \dfrac{1}{15}$

$\dfrac{14}{15} \div \Box = \dfrac{14}{15}$

d) $\dfrac{40}{45} \div \Box = \dfrac{4}{45}$

$\dfrac{40}{45} \div \Box = \dfrac{5}{45}$

$\dfrac{40}{45} \div \Box = \dfrac{20}{45}$

$\dfrac{40}{45} \div \Box = \dfrac{8}{45}$

7 A snail travels $\frac{12}{15}$ km in 3 days. It travels the same distance each day.

What fraction of a km does the snail travel each day?

8 Max is dividing a fraction by a whole number.

He simplifies his answer. Work out the missing numbers.

$$\frac{\boxed{}}{18} \div 3 = \frac{2}{9} \qquad \frac{\boxed{}}{60} \div 4 = \frac{7}{30} \qquad \frac{\boxed{}}{24} \div 2 = \frac{3}{8}$$

Reflect

Danny says $\frac{10}{15} \div 5 = \frac{2}{3}$.

Explain the mistake Danny has made. What is the correct answer? Prove it.

Dividing a fraction by a whole number

1   **a)** Use the diagram to help you work out $\frac{3}{4} \div 2$.

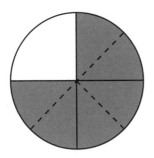

$$\frac{3}{4} \div 2 = \frac{\boxed{}}{8} \div 2 = \frac{\boxed{}}{8}$$

b) Use the diagram to help you work out $\frac{2}{5} \div 3$.

$$\frac{2}{5} \div 3 = \frac{\boxed{}}{15} \div 3 = \frac{\boxed{}}{15}$$

2   Use the diagrams to work out the divisions.

a)

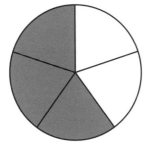

$$\frac{3}{5} \div 2 = \frac{\boxed{}}{10} \div 2 = \frac{\boxed{}}{10}$$

b)

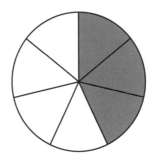

$$\frac{3}{7} \div 2 = \frac{\boxed{}}{\boxed{}} \div 2 = \frac{\boxed{}}{\boxed{}}$$

3 Complete these calculations.

a) $\dfrac{5}{8} \div 2 = \dfrac{\boxed{}}{16} \div 2$

   $= \dfrac{\boxed{}}{16}$

b) $\dfrac{4}{5} \div 3 = \dfrac{\boxed{}}{15} \div 3$

   $= \dfrac{\boxed{}}{\boxed{}}$

c) $\dfrac{5}{8} \div 3 = \dfrac{\boxed{}}{\boxed{}} \div \boxed{}$

   $=$

d) $\dfrac{3}{10} \div 4 = \dfrac{\boxed{}}{\boxed{}} \div \boxed{}$

   $=$

e) $\dfrac{2}{9} \div 5 = \dfrac{\boxed{}}{\boxed{}} \div \boxed{}$

   $=$

f) $\dfrac{5}{9} \div 2 = \dfrac{\boxed{}}{\boxed{}} \div \boxed{}$

   $=$

4 Complete these calculations. Give each answer in its simplest form.

a) $\dfrac{2}{5} \div 4 = \dfrac{\boxed{}}{20} \div 4$

   $= \dfrac{\boxed{}}{20} = \dfrac{\boxed{}}{10}$

b) $\dfrac{2}{6} \div 3 = \dfrac{\boxed{}}{18} \div 3$

   $= \dfrac{\boxed{}}{18} = \dfrac{\boxed{}}{\boxed{}}$

5 A bottle of milk is $\dfrac{4}{5}$ full. The milk is shared equally between 10 glasses.

What fraction of the bottle of milk will be in each glass?

6 Work out the values of the symbols.

$\frac{3}{8} \div 2 = \blacksquare$ $\qquad$ $\frac{4}{5} \div 2 = \bullet$ $\qquad$ $\frac{3}{4} \div \blacklozenge = \frac{3}{20}$ $\qquad$ $\frac{2}{3} \div \blacktriangle = \frac{1}{6}$

Work out these calculations.

a) $\blacksquare \div \blacklozenge = \dfrac{\boxed{}}{\boxed{}}$ $\qquad$ b) $\bullet \div \blacktriangle = \dfrac{\boxed{}}{\boxed{}}$ $\qquad$ c) $\bullet \div \blacklozenge = \dfrac{\boxed{}}{\boxed{}}$

Reflect

Describe how you would find $\frac{2}{7} \div 4$. Explain why you would use this method.

143

→ **Textbook 6A p196**

Four rules with fractions

1 Work out the perimeter of each shape.

a)

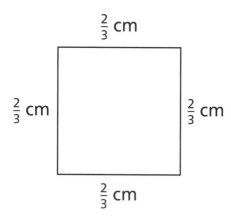

$\frac{2}{3} \times 4 = \dfrac{\boxed{}}{\boxed{}}$

$= \boxed{}\ \dfrac{\boxed{}}{\boxed{}}$

The perimeter is $\boxed{}\ \dfrac{\boxed{}}{\boxed{}}$ cm.

b)

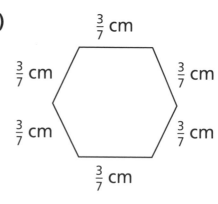

$\dfrac{\boxed{}}{\boxed{}} \times \boxed{} = \dfrac{\boxed{}}{\boxed{}}$

$= \boxed{}\ \dfrac{\boxed{}}{\boxed{}}$

The perimeter is $\boxed{}\ \dfrac{\boxed{}}{\boxed{}}$ cm.

2 Work out the area and perimeter of the rectangle.

$\frac{4}{5}$ cm

$\frac{2}{7}$ cm

144

3 Richard lives $\frac{3}{7}$ km from school.

Each day he walks to school and walks home.

How far does he walk in total from Monday to Friday?

4 Work out these calculations.

a) $\frac{1}{3} + \frac{1}{4} \times \frac{1}{3} = \dfrac{\boxed{}}{\boxed{}}$

b) $\frac{1}{5} \times \frac{2}{3} \div 2 = \dfrac{\boxed{}}{\boxed{}}$

5 This shape is made of a square and an isosceles triangle. The perimeter of the whole shape is $\frac{7}{10}$ metres.

How long is each side of the square?

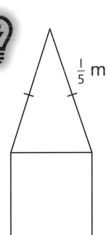

$\frac{1}{5}$ m

6 Here are three identical rectangles. A part of each rectangle is shaded.

What fraction of the middle rectangle is shaded?

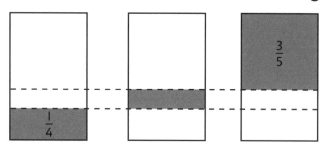

I will say that the whole area of the rectangle is 1.

Reflect

Max worked out $\frac{1}{2} + \frac{1}{4} \times \frac{1}{2}$.

What mistake did Max make?

What is the correct answer?

First I did $\frac{1}{2} + \frac{1}{4} = \frac{3}{4}$.

Then I did $\frac{3}{4} \times \frac{1}{2} = \frac{3}{8}$.

Max

Calculating fractions of amounts

1 There are 48 buttons in a box. $\frac{5}{6}$ of the buttons are red and the rest are blue.

48 buttons

How many buttons are blue?

2 Andy won £720 in a competition. He gave $\frac{1}{3}$ of the money to his sister.

How much money did he have left?

3 Kate and Ebo each bake 60 cookies for charity. Kate sells $\frac{2}{3}$ of her cookies. Ebo sells $\frac{7}{12}$ of his cookies.

Who sells more cookies? How many more?

4 A box of chocolates costs £4·80. Sofia pays $\frac{4}{5}$ and Holly pays the rest.

How much more does Sofia pay than Holly?

5 Work out these calculations.

a) $\frac{9}{10}$ of 170 km = ☐ km

c) $\frac{1}{7}$ of 0·35 km = ☐ _____

b) $\frac{1}{5}$ of 3 hours = ☐ _____

I wonder if I can change the units in parts b) and c).

6 Use <, > or = to complete the sentences. Use a diagram to help you.

a) $\frac{3}{7}$ of 70 $\bigcirc$ $\frac{5}{7}$ of 70

b) $\frac{2}{5}$ of 45 $\bigcirc$ $\frac{2}{3}$ of 45

7 Amelia bakes 36 biscuits. She keeps $\frac{1}{3}$ of the biscuits.

CHALLENGE

Amelia gives $\frac{5}{8}$ of the remaining biscuits to her dad and the rest to her mum.

How many biscuits does she give to her mum?

Reflect

Which question did you find the most challenging? How did you work it out?

→ Textbook 6A p204

Problem solving – fractions of amounts

 $\frac{1}{3}$ of the animals in a field are sheep. There are 17 sheep in the field.

How many animals are in the field?

17 sheep = $\frac{1}{3}$ of the animals

17 × ☐ = ☐

There are ☐ animals in the field.

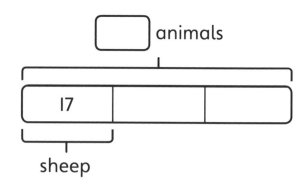

☐ animals

| 17 | | |

sheep

2 $\frac{5}{6}$ of a number is 60. What is the number?

3 Danny spends $\frac{2}{5}$ of his pocket money on a magazine. The magazine costs £3. How much pocket money does he get?

4 Last week, Toshi spent £42 on a food shop. This is $\frac{1}{7}$ of his weekly wage.

Holly spent £54. This is $\frac{2}{9}$ of her weekly wage.

Who earns more money per week? How much more?

5 Use a diagram to work out the missing numbers.

a) $\frac{1}{4}$ of ☐ = 20

c) $180 = \frac{9}{10}$ of ☐

b) $\frac{3}{4}$ of ☐ = 48

d) $\frac{1}{6}$ of ☐ = $\frac{2}{3}$ of 27

6 Zac is thinking of a number. What number is Zac thinking of?

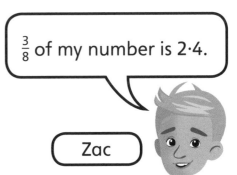

$\frac{3}{8}$ of my number is 2·4.

Zac

7 **a)** On Monday, Alex reads $\frac{1}{4}$ of a book. On Tuesday, she reads $\frac{3}{5}$ of the book. She has 18 pages left to read. How many pages are in her book?

b) On Monday, Lee reads $\frac{1}{4}$ of a book. On Tuesday, he reads $\frac{3}{5}$ of the remaining pages. He has 18 pages left to read. How many pages are there in Lee's book?

Reflect

$\frac{3}{4}$ of 60 = ☐ $\frac{3}{4}$ of ☐ = 60

What is the same? What is different? Work out the missing numbers.

End of unit check

My journal

1. Choose two calculations from the table.

$\frac{1}{5} \times 3$	$\frac{1}{3} \div 4$	$\frac{2}{3} \div 4$	$\frac{7}{10} + \frac{2}{5} \times \frac{1}{2}$
$\frac{2}{3} \times \frac{3}{8}$	$\frac{4}{5} \div 2$	$\frac{7}{10} + \frac{2}{5}$	$\frac{7}{10} \times \frac{2}{5} + \frac{1}{2}$

Write down the steps involved in working out each calculation.

Explain to your partner how you worked out each calculation. Does your partner agree with your methods?

Power check

How do you feel about your work in this unit?

Power puzzle

1 Work out the value of each letter.

A	B	C	D	E	F	G	H
36							

$\frac{1}{2}$ of $\boxed{A}$ = $\boxed{B}$

$\frac{2}{5}$ of $\boxed{D}$ = $\frac{1}{3}$ of $\boxed{B}$

$\frac{2}{5} \times \frac{1}{3} \times \boxed{D}$ = $\boxed{G}$

$\frac{2}{3}$ of $\boxed{C}$ = $\boxed{B}$

$\frac{3}{10} \times \boxed{D}$ = $\boxed{E}$

$\frac{1}{10} \div \boxed{G}$ = $\boxed{H}$

$\frac{\boxed{F}}{9}$ of $\boxed{C}$ = $\boxed{B}$ + $\frac{1}{3}$ of $\boxed{B}$

Can you make up your own problems like this to challenge your partner?

2 A, B and C are three points on a number line. C is $\frac{2}{3}$ of the distance between A and B.

A   C↓   B
30   210

Write the value of C on the number line.

Plotting coordinates in the first quadrant

1 Plot the following points on the grid.

A at (2,3)

B at (8,1)

C at (5,7)

D at (0,4)

E at (7,0)

F at (3·5,6)

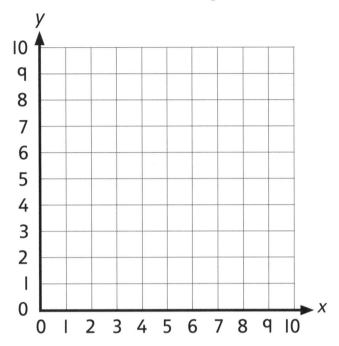

2 Write the coordinates of all the points.

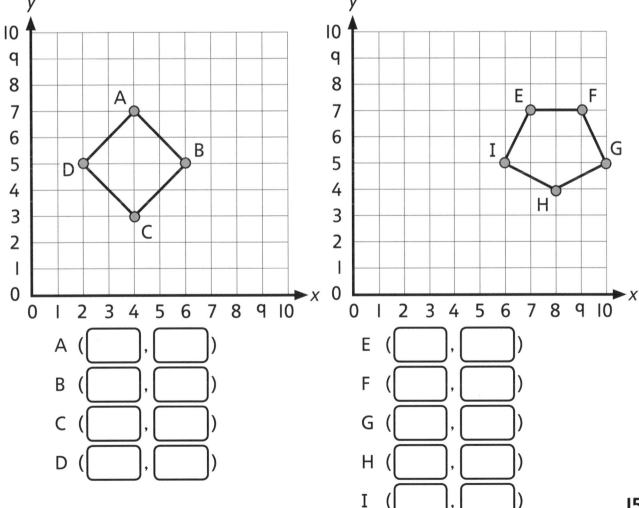

A (☐ , ☐)

B (☐ , ☐)

C (☐ , ☐)

D (☐ , ☐)

E (☐ , ☐)

F (☐ , ☐)

G (☐ , ☐)

H (☐ , ☐)

I (☐ , ☐)

155

3 **a)** Line AB is part of a square.

What could the coordinates of the other two vertices of this square be?

(⬜ , ⬜)

(⬜ , ⬜)

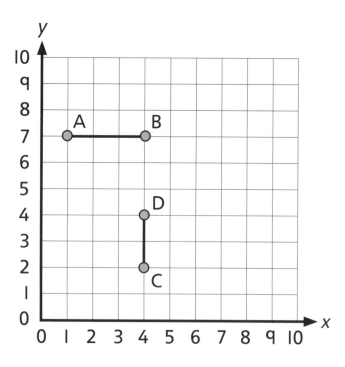

b) CD is the width of a rectangle. The length of the rectangle is twice the width. What could the coordinates of the other two vertices be?

(⬜ , ⬜)

(⬜ , ⬜)

4 The line shown is one side of a square.

a) Draw the rest of the square.

b) What are the coordinates of the vertices of the square?

(⬜ , ⬜)

(⬜ , ⬜)

(⬜ , ⬜)

(⬜ , ⬜)

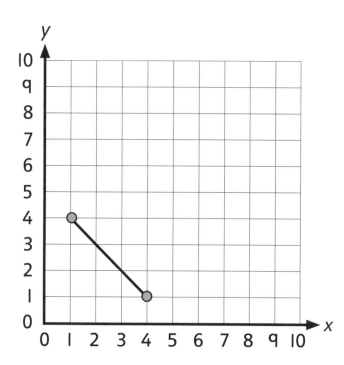

5 The sides of the three squares are all the same length.

Work out the coordinates of points A, B, C, D and E.

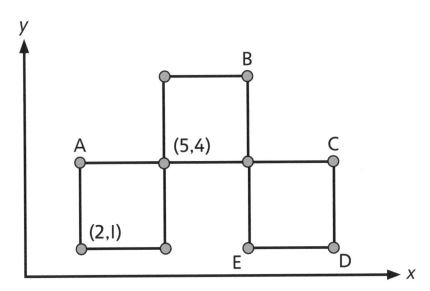

The coordinates of the points are:

Point A (⬜ , ⬜)

Point B (⬜ , ⬜)

Point C (⬜ , ⬜)

Point D (⬜ , ⬜)

Point E (⬜ , ⬜)

Reflect

If one of the coordinates of a point is 0, what does it tell you about the point?

→ **Textbook 6A p216**

Plotting coordinates

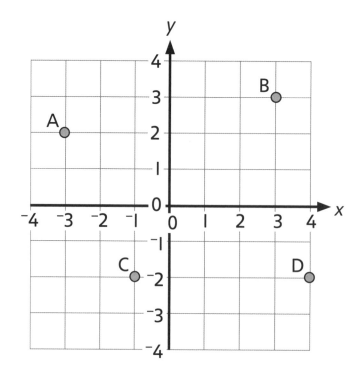

a) What are the coordinates of the points on the grid?

Point A (⬜ , ⬜)   Point C (⬜ , ⬜)

Point B (⬜ , ⬜)   Point D (⬜ , ⬜)

b) Now plot these coordinates on the grid.

Point E (⁻3,⁻2)

Point F (2,⁻1)

Point G (⁻1,3)

Point H (⁻3,0)

I know that the first number counts along the x-axis and that the second number counts up or down the y-axis.

2 The sets of coordinates below make shapes.

Shape A coordinates: (0,2), (3,2), (⁻1,⁻2), (4,⁻2)

Shape B coordinates: (⁻5,1), (⁻3,1), (⁻2,⁻1), (⁻3,⁻2), (⁻5,⁻2), (⁻6,⁻1)

Plot the coordinates on the grid and connect them to work out the shapes.

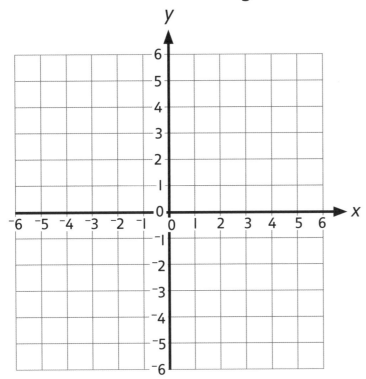

Shape A is a _____ .

Shape B is a _____ .

3 Lucy says, 'It doesn't matter which way round you write coordinates in brackets. You would always get the same point when you plotted them.' Is Lucy correct? Why?

_____

_____

_____

_____

4 Mia has plotted three points of a rectangle: (⁻3,3), (4,3), (4,⁻1).

What point does Mia need to plot to complete her rectangle?

CHALLENGE

I will use the grid to plot the coordinates I do know.

Mia needs to plot the point (☐ , ☐) to complete her rectangle.

Reflect

Lily says: 'It is harder to plot coordinates in all four quadrants than to plot them in just one.' Do you agree with her? Why?

_____

_____

_____

_____

Plotting translations and reflections

1 Complete the reflections. Draw your answers on the coordinates grid.

a) Reflect shape A in the *x*-axis.

b) Reflect shape B in the *x*-axis.

c) Reflect shape C in the *y*-axis.

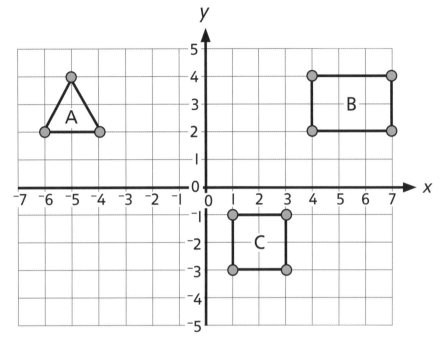

2 Complete the translations. Draw your answers on the coordinate grid.

a) Translate the rectangle 4 down and 3 to the right.

b) Translate the irregular hexagon 5 up and 6 to the left.

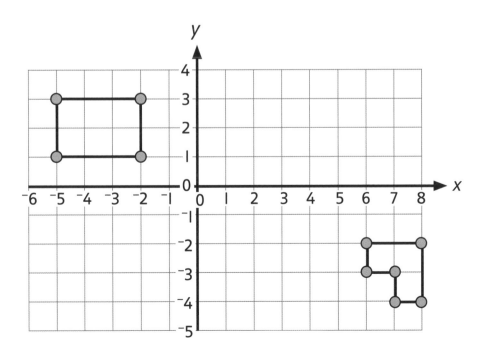

3 Complete the following sentences.

Shape A has been _____ in _____ to make shape B.

Shape C has been reflected in _____ to make shape D.

Shape _____ has been _____ [ ] units

_____ and [ ] units

_____ to make Shape F.

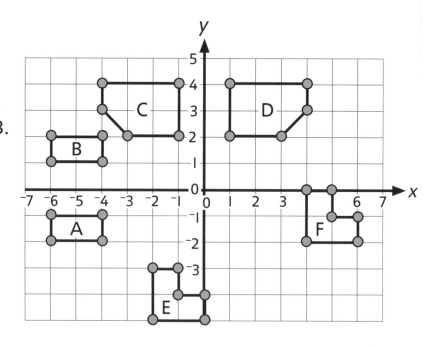

4 Reflect this shape in the diagonal line. Draw your answer on the grid.

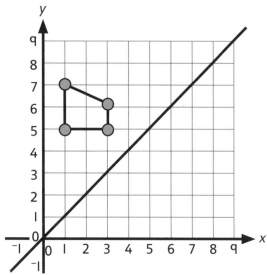

5 This rectangle is reflected in the y-axis.

Write the coordinates of the vertices of the reflected rectangle:

([ ] , [ ]), ([ ] , [ ]),

([ ] , [ ]), ([ ] , [ ])

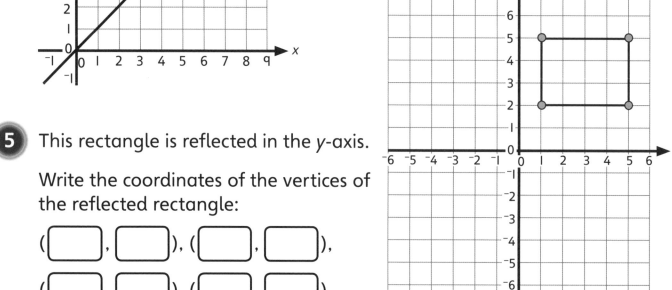

CHALLENGE

6 **a)** Reflect this shape in the y-axis. Then translate it 3 to the right and 2 down.

b) Now translate the first shape 3 to the right and 2 down, and then reflect it in the y-axis.

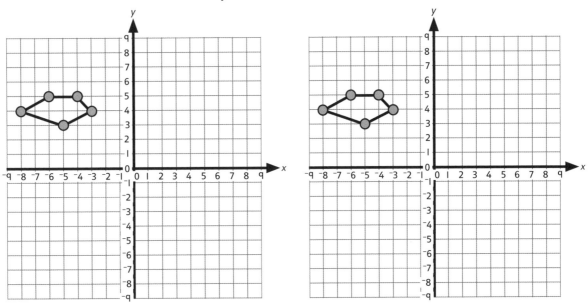

Do you get the same answer for a) and b)? Why or why not?

I do / do not get the same answers (circle as appropriate) because

_____

Reflect

Charlie says: 'When you reflect or translate a shape, the reflected or translated shape is identical to the shape you started with.' Is Charlie correct?

Discuss with your partner and write your answer here.

_____

_____

→ Textbook 6A p224

Reasoning about shapes with coordinates

1 Two vertices of a square are at the coordinates (⁻2,1) and (⁻2,⁻1).

What are the coordinates of the other two vertices of the square?

One set of possible coordinates for the other vertices are:

(☐,☐), (☐,☐)

Another set of possible coordinates for the other vertices are:

(☐,☐), (☐,☐)

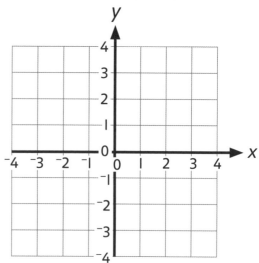

2 Squares P and Q are shown.

The coordinates of A are (1,6) and the coordinates of B are (5,6).

Square P was translated 4 units left and 8 units down to make square Q.

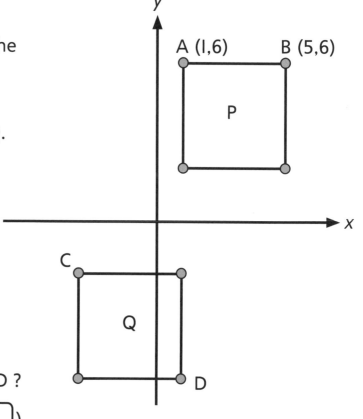

What are the coordinates of C and D ?

C (☐,☐)   D (☐,☐)

3 Here are two identical isosceles triangles. AC = BC and DF = EF.

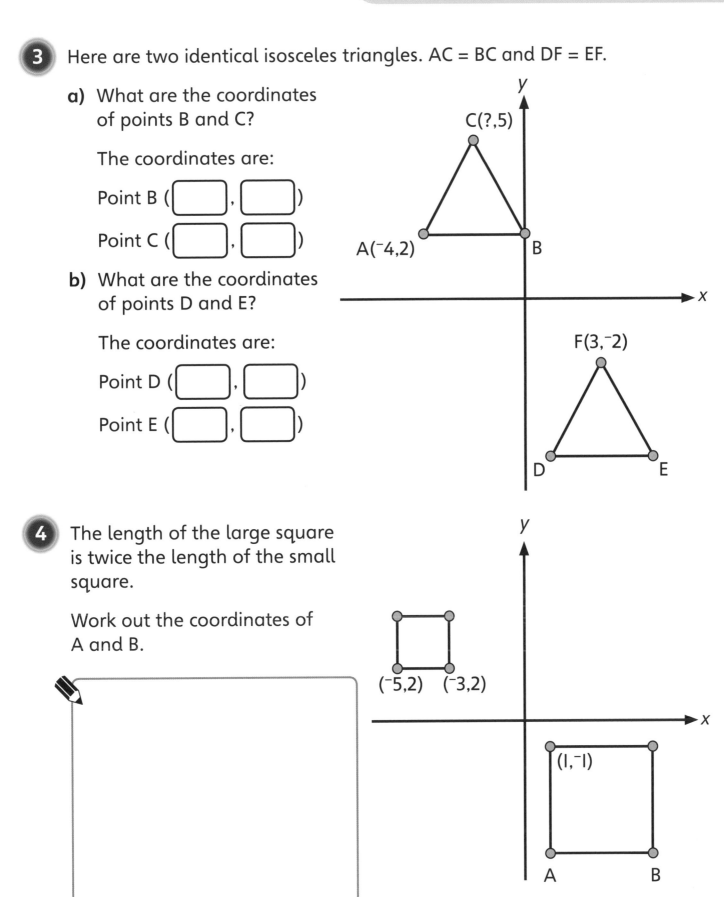

a) What are the coordinates of points B and C?

The coordinates are:

Point B (⬚ , ⬚)

Point C (⬚ , ⬚)

C(?,5)

A(⁻4,2)

B

b) What are the coordinates of points D and E?

The coordinates are:

Point D (⬚ , ⬚)

Point E (⬚ , ⬚)

F(3,⁻2)

D   E

4 The length of the large square is twice the length of the small square.

Work out the coordinates of A and B.

(⁻5,2)   (⁻3,2)

(1,⁻1)

A   B

5 Below are three identical parallelograms.

Work out the coordinates of points A, B, C and D.

The coordinates of the labelled points are:

Point A (⬚ , ⬚)   Point C (⬚ , ⬚)

Point B (⬚ , ⬚)   Point D (⬚ , ⬚)

CHALLENGE

> Remember to use what you know about the properties of a parallelogram to help you.

(−3,5) (2,5)

(−2,2)

A

B

D

C

Reflect

Which problem did you find the most challenging in this lesson? Why did you find it challenging? How did you solve it?

End of unit check

My journal

1 The shape on this coordinate grid is a square.

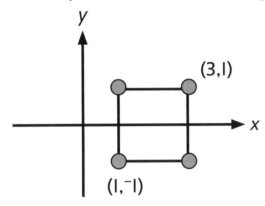

Kate says: 'It is not possible to reflect this shape in the *y*-axis with the information we have in the diagram.'

Is Kate correct?

Yes / No (circle as appropriate)

Explain how you know:

_____

_____

_____

_____

_____

2 The point on the grid is a vertex of a rectangle.

The rectangle has side lengths of 5 units and 3 units.

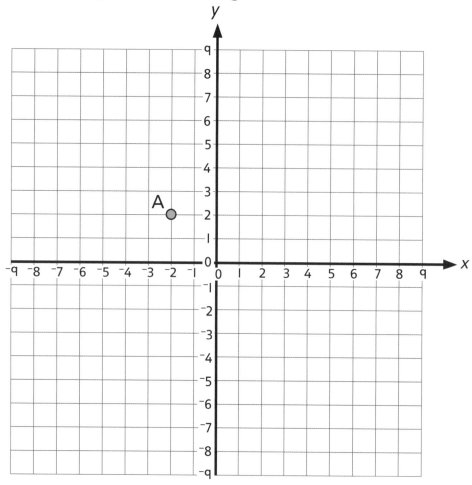

Draw all the possible rectangles on the grid.

Write all the possible coordinates of the other vertices of this rectangle.

_____

_____

_____

Power check

How do you feel about your work in this unit?

?

Power play

How can you use the properties of squares to help you find the other vertices of your partner's squares? Is it easier or harder if your partner's squares overlap? Why?

Square battleships

You need a partner to play this game.

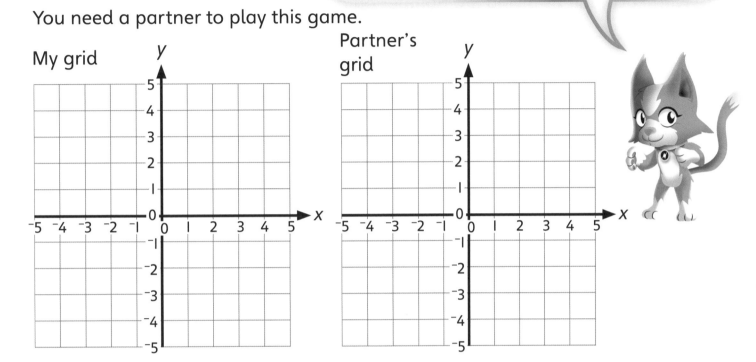

My grid

Partner's grid

How to play:

1. Draw three squares on 'My grid'. Your partner should draw three squares on 'My grid' in their own book.

2. Take it in turns to guess the coordinates of the vertices of each other's squares.

   Each time you guess, your partner should tell you if you have 'hit' (you have guessed a vertex correctly) or 'missed' (you have not guessed a vertex correctly).

   If you have a 'hit', you should mark this vertex on the 'Partner's grid' in your book.

   If you have a 'hit', you get another go.

3. The game ends when one player has found all the vertices of the other player's squares.

My power points

Put a tick against the topics you have learnt about. Show how confident you are with each one by giving it a number on a scale of 1 to 3.

1 = not at all confident;
2 = getting there;
3 = very confident

Unit 1

I have learnt how to ...

☐ Read and write numbers to 10,000,000 ☐

☐ Partition, compare and order numbers up to 10,000,000 ☐

☐ Round numbers ☐

☐ Work with negative numbers ☐

Unit 2

I have learnt how to ...

☐ Use written methods for addition and subtraction ☐

☐ Use column multiplication ☐

☐ Use different written methods for division ☐

☐ Check strategies for our calculations ☐

Unit 3

I have learnt how to ...

☐ Find common factors and multiples ☐

☐ Understand prime, square and cube numbers ☐

☐ Use operations in the correct order ☐

☐ Solve mental calculations ☐

Unit 4

I have learnt how to …

☐ Simplify fractions ☐

☐ Compare and order fractions ☐

☐ Add and subtract fractions including mixed numbers ☐

☐ Solve problems involving adding and subtracting fractions ☐

Unit 5

I have learnt how to …

☐ Multiply any fraction by a whole number or another fraction ☐

☐ Divide a fraction by a whole number ☐

☐ Solve problems involving all four operations with fractions ☐

☐ Solve problems involving a fraction of an amount ☐

Unit 6

I have learnt how to …

☐ Use coordinates to describe the position of a point on a grid ☐

☐ Use coordinates with positive or negative values ☐

☐ Solve problems with shapes on a coordinate grid ☐

☐ Plot and read translations and reflections on a coordinate grid ☐

Keep up the good work!

Notes

Notes

Squared paper

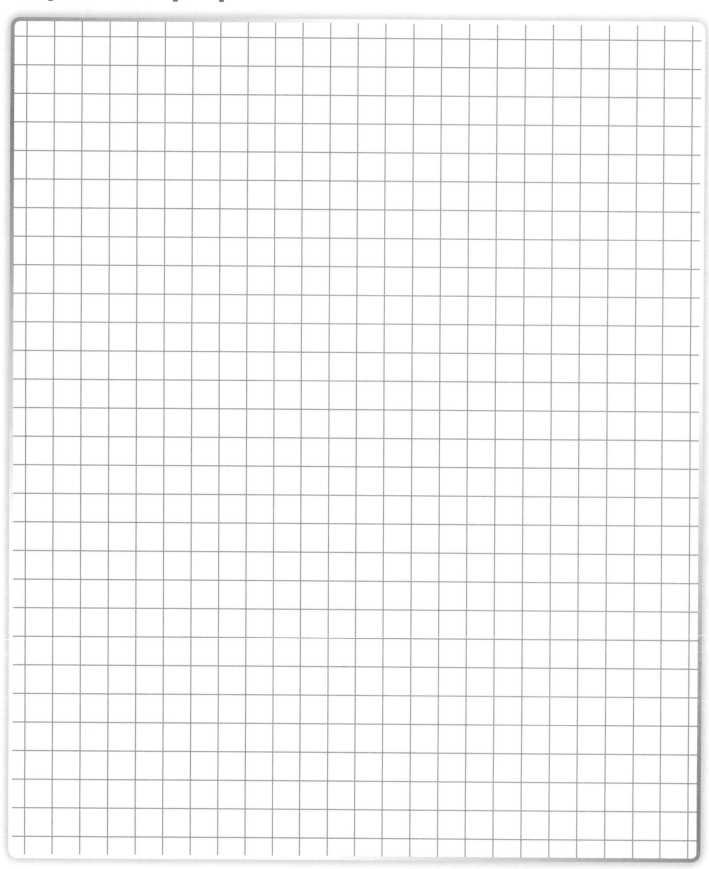

Squared paper

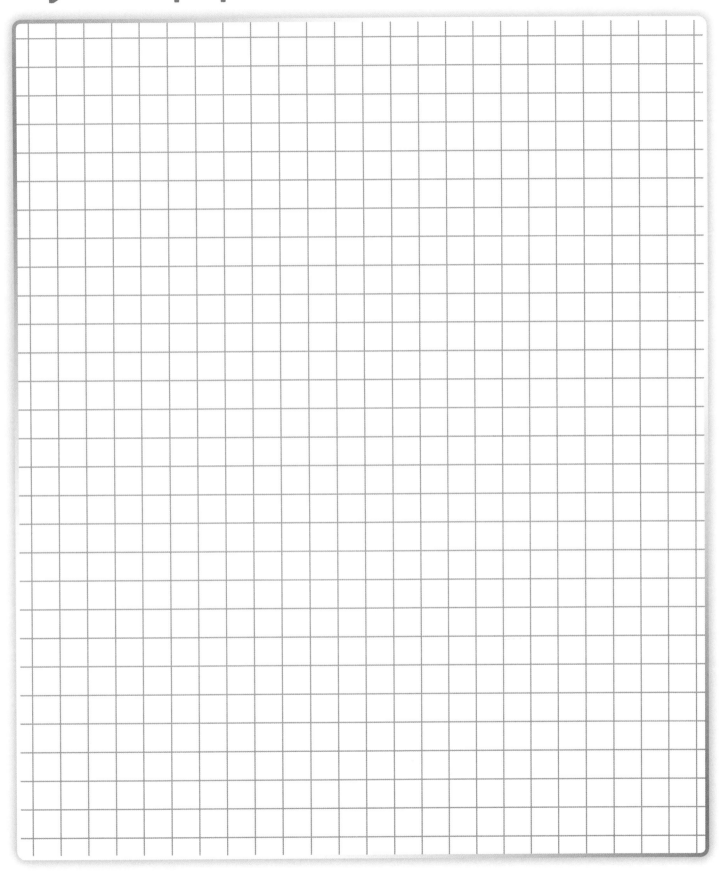

Square dotted paper